W elcome to the Haliburton edition of the Fishing Ontario Series. This series has been designed as the most complete angling guide on the best fishing locations in the province. The coloured depth charts combined with invaluable information on such things as access, facilities, stocking and fish species will allow you to choose that ideal lake or water body for your fishing adventure. The amazing feature of this guidebook is that it provides you with detailed information on where on the water to fish. This information is invaluable to increasing your success and is especially important to anglers visiting a lake or river for the first time.

The Haliburton region has long been a popular fishing destination and is riddled with both small and large lakes offering boundless fishing opportunities. Visitors to the region will find hundreds of beautiful lakes and water bodies to explore, including the lakes of the Haliburton Forest Reserve and the Leslie M. Frost Centre. The region is comprised of mainly cold water lakes, as the region is a highland area similar to the terrain of Algonquin Provincial Park. The cool, deep lakes are prime habitat for trout species such as lake trout and brook trout. The rocky terrain of many Haliburton lakes also makes a fantastic environment for smallmouth bass. Feisty smallmouth can be found in many of the lakes and always put up a fantastic fight when hooked. From the deep holding lake trout, to the rocky shorelines where rod bending smallmouth can be found, Haliburton offers a limitless array of fishing possibilities.

In this book, we have provided detailed depth charts to over 90 of the best lakes and water bodies found in the Haliburton area. To ensure you have a successful trip, we have also provided information on access, facilities, stocking, fishing hints and

surrounding lakes.

This region of Ontario offers a well developed system of roads, providing easy access to most of the area lakes. There is also a good collection of harder to reach lakes in the region that require a 4wd vehicle or are only accessible by trail or portage. For more detailed access information to all the lakes in Haliburton, we recommend consulting the Backroad Mapbook, Ontario Cottage Country. The Backroad Mapbook provides very detailed maps along with information on everything from camping areas to other fishing opportunities. It is the perfect compliment to the Fishing Ontario book for the Haliburton area.

No other source combines such detailed information on the best fishing lakes in the Haliburton area. Whether you are visiting the region for the first time or simply looking for a new lake to fish, we are certain you will find this book an invaluable guide.

FISHING Ontario

DIRECTORS
Russell Mussio
Wesley Mussio
Penny Stainton-Mussio

COVER & LAYOUT
Farnaz Faghihi

PRODUCTION
Adrian Brugge
Alfred Berger
Shawn Caswell
Farnaz Faghihi
Brett Firth
Grace Teo
Dale Tober
Heather Yetman

WRITERS
Jason Marleau
Russell Mussio
Wesley Mussio

National Library of Canada Cataloguing in Publication Data

Marleau, Jason, 1972-
Mussio Ventures presents Fishing Ontario : Haliburton.
Written by Jason Marleau and Russell Mussio.
Includes index.
ISBN 1-894556-26-7

1. Fishing--Ontario--Haliburton (County)--Guidebooks. 2. Haliburton (Ont. : County)--Guidebooks. I. Mussio, Russell, 1969- II. Title. III. Title: Fishing Ontario : Haliburton.
SH572.O5M359 2003   799.1'1'0971361
C2003-911017-6

Published by:

232 Anthony Court
New Westminster, B.C. V3L 5T5
P. (604) 438-3474   F. (604) 438-3470
E-mail: info@backroadmapbooks.com
www.backroadmapbooks.com
Copyright © 2003 Mussio Ventures Ltd.

Disclaimer

The lake charts contained in this book are not intended for navigational purposes. Uncharted rocks and shoals may exist.

Mussio Ventures Ltd. does not warrant that the information contained in this guide is correct. Therefore, please be careful when using this or any source to plan and carry out your outdoor recreation activity. Also note that travelling on logging roads and trails is inherently dangerous, and you may encounter poor road conditions, unexpected traffic, poor visibility, and low or no road/trail maintenance. Please use extreme caution when travelling logging roads and trails.

Please refer to the Ontario Recretaional Fishing Regulations for closures and restrictions. It is your responsibility to know when and where closures and restrictions apply.

Table of Contents

The Lakes

Haliburton Lakes

The Haliburton area was slowly settled in the mid to late 1800's, as settlers were enticed with promises of large, cheap land plots. The terrain was rugged, with the rocky forested hills dominating the landscape. Logging and trapping became the mainstay of the region as the forests were aggressively harvested to feed the needs of a growing country and overseas interests. Over a century later, the Haliburton area has been established as a popular year round tourism area. Visitors flock to the region each year to escape their urban settings to the mystique of the Haliburton Highlands. From popular cottage destination lakes, to scenic backcountry retreats, Haliburton is a fantastic place to explore.

The Haliburton region is a pocket of area set just south of the famous Algonquin Park and stretches south to the Kawarthas. The western border stretches from around Highway 28 eastward to near Highway 35. As part of the Canadian Shield, the Haliburton region is a vast expanse of rolling forested hills, with many lakes dominated by rugged rocky shorelines. Far removed from the era of logging, coniferous and deciduous trees blanket the region, creating a truly magnificent autumn display of colour. The area is also home to a variety of animals that are typically found in the wilds of Ontario including de   oons and an abundance of waterfowl. Larger animals, such as bears and moose, rarely frequent the more developed areas but can be found throughout the region.

Some of the more popular lakes in the region are found along the main access highways. Many lakes in this region are home to cottages and, hence, can be quite busy during the summer months. The main advantage of the more popular lakes is that they usually offer maintained boat launch facilities and amenities. For a more remote type setting, look for those hidden, hard to get to lakes in the sections between the main highways, like the area north of Highway 118 and Highway 121. Although Haliburton is well serviced by roadways, a high clearance and/or 4wd vehicle is recommended if you do head into the backcountry.

The Haliburton region is comprised of mainly cold water lakes where trout species are king. Along with an aggressive stocking program, many lakes still hold natural populations of lake trout and brook trout. Smallmouth bass were introduced decades ago into many area lakes and naturally regenerating populations can be found in numerous lakes alongside other sportfish species. In big open waters bodies, trolling is a popular method of finding larger sportfish such as lake trout. On the more remote, smaller lakes, casting from a boat or canoe can be a relaxing and productive method.

The majority of angling and boating traffic on all lakes in the Haliburton region is found in the months of July and August. During the early spring and fall period, the bustling nature of the region decreases dramatically. In general, the months of May and October can be desolate despite the fact these can be productive fishing months.

Winter sets in around mid-November and ice is often formed on lakes by mid-December. Ice fishing used to be a widespread tradition in the Haliburton area; however, in order to reduce fishing pressure on many lakes, the season is now limited if not closed entirely. Lakes that still offer ice fishing are often dotted with small ice fishing huts throughout the season. Ice on lakes in the Haliburton area is usually melted off by mid-April.

Please Note: There are angling regulations in effect on all water bodies in Ontario in order to preserve the future of the resource. Some of the more specific regulations may include bait bans, special limits, slot size restrictions and closures. Penalty for breaking these regulations can include heavy fines, seizure of equipment and/or imprisonment. Always check the annual Ontario Recreational Fishing Regulations Summary before fishing!

Haliburton Fish Species

Largemouth Bass

Largemouth bass are found sporadically in the Haliburton region, and often are mainly found in lakes along with smallmouth bass. In lakes with largemouth bass, top water lures and flies can create excellent action. Plastic jigs or any minnow imitation lure or fly can also be productive. Largemouth bass are readily adaptable to warm water lakes and generally grow larger than its cousin, the smallmouth bass. The Ontario record largemouth bass is 4.7 kg (10.43 lbs).

Rainbow Trout

Rainbow trout are native to the Pacific Northwest and by the late 1800's had been stocked into the Great Lakes. Today rainbow trout have also been introduced into many inland lakes in Ontario, although spawning success is limited. The cool waters of several Haliburton lakes have made fine environments for stocked rainbow. It is not uncommon to find fish in the 8 kg (17.6 lbs) range in the Great Lakes, while inland lake sizes of rainbow trout usually average 35-45 cm (14-18 in). Fly fishing can be a very productive method for inland rainbow but small spinners and spoons also produce results. The Ontario record rainbow trout is 13.2 kg (29.12 lbs).

Smallmouth Bass

Smallmouth bass are found frequently in Haliburton and are the close cousin of the largemouth bass. Smallmouth bass are not indigenous to most lakes of the region, as they were readily introduced into many systems over the past thirty to forty years. The smallmouth has a reputation of putting up a great fight when hooked, and can be a very aggressive feeder at times. The smallmouth readily strikes jigs, spinners, spoons and other fast moving lures that look like a good meal. The smallmouth can be found around structure such as shoals, islands and under water drop-offs. The Ontario record smallmouth bass is 4.5kg (9.84 lbs).

Lake Trout

Lake trout can grow to sizes exceeding 6 kg (13 lbs), although in smaller lakes the average is about 2-3 kg (4-7 lbs). These big fish can be found near the surface in spring when the temperature level throughout the lake is generally constant. Fish of all sizes can be caught with regular gear virtually anywhere in the lake. As summer approaches lakers retreat to colder water and to depths that require down rigging equipment to find them. Spoons, spinners, or anything that imitates the lake trout's main food source, the minnow, are good choices when angling for lakers. Lake trout continue to be one of the most heavily fished species in the province and in the Haliburton area. Changes in the fishing seasons and other regulations have made strides in helping sustain natural lake trout fisheries in the Haliburton area. To further aid populations, it is imperative that the use of catch and release fishing becomes a popular angling practice. The Ontario record lake trout is 28.6 kg (63 lbs).

Brook Trout

Brook trout are also known as speckled trout due to the red spots with blue halos on their sides and are native to a number of streams and lakes in the Haliburton area. Brookies are often a fickle and difficult fish to catch and can sometimes be 'spooked' by even talking too loud on a lake. Lake brook trout can be found to 1 kg (2.2 lbs) and sometimes larger. One of the most effective methods of angling for brookies is fly fishing.

Small spoons and spinners tipped with worms can also be productive, especially when fishing trout through the ice. Unfortunately, due to fishing pressure, the majority of native brook trout lakes in the region must now be stocked in order to offer productive angling opportunities. The Ontario record brook trout is 6.58 kg (14.5 lbs).

Walleye

Walleye are also known as pickerel and are perhaps the most prized sportfish in Ontario. The walleye's diet is made up of mainly baitfish, although they do take leeches and other grub like creatures. Jigs are the lure of choice for walleye either through the ice or during open water season. Walleye travel in loose schools and once you find them, you should be able to catch more than one. Jigging in set locations or trolling slowly along weed beds can entice strikes. Walleye are most active during the darker times of day; hence, early morning and evening are the most productive periods. Over the past few years, Eastern Ontario has seen a decline in its native walleye stocks. New regulations such as slot sizes and size minimums should help to sustain the current fishery. The Ontario record walleye is 10.1 kgs (22.25 lbs).

Northern Pike

Northern pike are the close cousin of the muskellunge and inhabit numerous lakes, from warmer murky lakes to even some of the more cool and clear water bodies in Haliburton. Pike can be quite aggressive at times and readily strike fast moving spoons, and spinners. Northern pike average about 1-3 kg (2-7 lbs) although can be found over 8 kg (17.6 lbs) in size in larger water bodies. The main food source for this predator is other fish, although colourful spoons or flies can be very productive baits. Ontario's record northern pike is 19.11 kg (42 lbs).

Muskellunge

Otherwise known as 'musky', this warm water predator feeds mainly on other fish and various small mammals. Muskellunge is the largest freshwater sportfish species in Ontario and can reach over 16 kg (35 lbs) in size on occasion. The most effective method for finding these large fish is by trolling long plugs and lures in calm bays where they often cruise for food. Fall is a productive time of year for these large fish. The Ontario record muskellunge weighed 29.5 kg (65 lbs).

Splake

Splake are sporadically stocked in the Haliburton area to reduce pressure on native trout lakes and to enhance angling opportunities. The species is a sterile cross between lake trout and brook trout and was developed specifically to stock lakes uninhabited by other trout species. Splake grow very rapidly similar to brook trout and to sizes similar to lake trout. Characteristic to both lake trout and brook trout, splake are most active in winter and in spring just after ice off. Similar to lake trout, they will strike shiny spoons and spinners and retreat to deeper water as summer approaches.

Fishing Techniques

Spincasting

The most popular angling method used in Ontario today is spincasting. Essentially, spincasting is the process of casting a line from a rod with a spinning reel. The spincasting set up is quite simple, making it easy for anyone to learn how to fish and have fun at it.

Equipment

There are a number of variations of spinning type reels available on the market today, although the two main spin reels are the closed face reel and the open face reel.

The difference between the two reels is quite basic. The line and action of the closed face reel is encased in order to help prevent tangling of the line and is cast by the simple point and click of a button on the reel. This type of reel has become the reel of choice of professional and recreational anglers over the past few years and has many advantages, most notably the ease of operation. One drawback is that the access to the line on the reel is limited.

Open face reels offer the angler full access to the line on the reel and control of the cast. The angler can actually hold the line with the index finger during the cast, aiding (or perhaps hindering) in the control of the cast. An advantage of this type of reel is mainly the access to the line, as more subtle flip type casts are often easier with this type of reel. One drawback of the open face reel is that it takes more work to throw a cast and tangling can be a problem with cheaper versions.

Basically, both reels can be used in almost any situation; therefore, the type of reel you choose to use should be based on personal preference.

Spincasting Lures

At any of your local tackle shops, you will find a seemingly endless array of tackle. From the endless versions of the spinner to the simple jig head and body, it can be a confusing decision. Here is a quick rundown of the lures and what they are mainly used for:

Spinners

There are a wide variety of spinners available. One of the main brand names for spinners is Mepps or Blue Fox, although there are countless variations and brands that all produce results. The spinner is a versatile lure proving successful for trout, bass and pike on occasion. The fast action of any spinner lure is very active and is usually worked quickly within about the 1-3 m (3-10 ft) depth range.

Spoons

Spoons come in a mix of sizes and colours. Spoons are more commonly used when fishing for pike and trout; however, they can be productive for other species as well. For pike, the larger presentations with brighter colours, like red or yellow, are the spoons of choice. For trout, smaller silver or gold spoons can be productive with shades of blue, or green. A popular brand name for trout spoons is the Little Cleo, while the Red Devil is a long heralded pike spoon.

Jigs

Jigs are made up of a weighted head and plastic body. Both the head and body come in a wide range of colours, shapes and sizes. As with any lure, the key to finding the right shape, size or colour is done mainly through trial and error. Jigs work well for bass and are a favourite lure of walleye anglers. The single hook nature of the jig also works as an effective anti snag type lure. A jig can be worked effectively through weeds, unlike most other lures.

Crankbaits

This type of lure is essentially a piece of painted plastic shaped to wobble when reeled through the water. As with any lure, there are hundreds of different crankbaits on the market. The lure can be productive for a wide variety of sportfish, but most notably for, walleye, pike and bass. The main advantage of any crankbait is its unique movement ability.

Top Water Lures

Some of the most exciting fishing is done with top water lures. Top water lures skim the surface of the water to entice fish to grab the lure from the surface of the lake. Top water lures can be quite effective for northern pike, smallmouth bass and largemouth bass. One of the old time favourite brands of top water lures is the Jitterbug.

Fly Fishing

Fly Fishing is slowly becoming more popular in Ontario as anglers look to a more challenging method in catching sportfish. Many anglers are put aback by the seemingly difficult nature of fly fishing; however, once learned, it is actually quite easy. Ardent fly anglers often boast of better success than their spincasting counterparts.

Fly Rods and Reels

Basically, there are three parts to a fly fishing outfit: the rod, the reel and the line. Rods come in a variety of lengths and weights, depending on your

size and the size of the species you intend to fish. As an example, a 9 ft, 6 weight rod would be an ideal set up for everything from bass to trout up to about 5 kg (11 lb) in size. The longer the rod, the easier it is to cast the fly line, however, this has limitations. The heavier the rod, like an 8 weight, the larger the species of fish you can fish for and vice versa. Many experienced fly anglers will have at least two if not three or more rods of different size and weight in order to maximize their fishing experience. Essentially, a smaller size and weight rod would be used for stream fishing small trout, while the longer heavier rod would be used for bigger species like northern pike or big fighting bass.

Fly Lines

There are basically three main types of fly lines; the floating line, sinking line and sink tip line. Floating line is used to fish top water flies and lures as it sits on top of the water to present the fly on the surface. Sinking line sinks to the depths of the lake in order to present streamer type flies or other subsurface type flies. Sink tip line is a combination of sinking and floating line where just the end of the fly line sinks. This type of line has a number of advantages, one being the ability to present sub surface flies while retaining the visibility of the fly line on the surface. This helps dramatically in spotting strikes, especially when fishing for trout.

Trout Flies

A few of the more popular trout flies used in Eastern Ontario lakes are the Muddler Minnow, leech pattern and multi purpose nymph. The Muddler Minnow is the pattern made famous in Ontario for its success with brook trout. The fly imitates a minnow in distress, the ideal meal for a big brookie. Leeches are a part of lake environments in Eastern Ontario and are a good fly for slow trolling the deeper portions of lakes in summer. All lakes are full of various insect larvae, such as caddis, mosquito and damsel fly larvae that are the main food source for most trout. Various nymph patterns that imitate this larvae can be very effective when fishing for rainbow and brook trout.

Fly fishing is not a popular method for lake trout but during spring it can be quite productive. Streamer pattern flies that imitate baitfish can be great for attracting the catch of a lifetime.

Bass and Pike Flies

The most exciting fly pattern used for both northern pike and bass is the popper. Poppers are surface flies that can be found in a variety of colours, patterns and sizes. Poppers hop along the top of the water and are great at stirring up aggressive bass and pike. Streamer patterns in colours such as white, red and yellow can also produce for both pike and bass. Many bass and pike streamer patterns are often tied with a weedless hook to aid travel through weed areas where many of the big ones hide out. A smallmouth bass fly that is quickly attracting acclaim is the crayfish pattern. Crayfish are tied many different ways, although when worked off bottom areas with a sinking line the results can be quite surprising.

Trolling

Trolling can be a very effective angling method, especially on larger water bodies. Trolling allows you to cover large areas of water, increasing your chances of finding success on a lake. Trolling is most often used when fishing for larger species, such as lake trout, northern pike, walleye, and muskellunge but that does not mean the odd bass will not hit your line.

Trolling speeds should vary to find an effective presentation and can be as slow as a wind drift. Trolling along drop-off areas in lakes usually increases your chances significantly. Also, try just along weed lines, as species such as walleye often cruise the same area in search of food. Spoons and plugs are the more popular lures when trolling, although variations such as a worm harness can be productive as well.

For deep trolling, as is often required during the summer for lake trout, down rigging equipment will enable you to troll your lure through holding areas. With the aid of a heavy weight, a downrigger will drop your line and lure to a desired depth in the lake. Down riggers are more common on large water bodies, such as Big Rideau Lake.

Ice Fishing

The ice fishing opportunities in the Haliburton region vary depending on the lake. Due to heavy fishing pressure, many lakes in the region have been permanently closed to ice fishing. Regardless, there remains a good selection of lakes to ice fish.

The standard set up for ice fishing involves a jig head and a minnow. This method is often productive for all species, although it has its limitations. An evolving ice fishing method is jigging small spoons and other attractant lures. Typically, this method does not produce numbers, but it does produce the big fish. If you do use live bait, be sure to check the regulations, as some lakes in the region have live bait ban restrictions in effect.

Ice fishing season typically begins on January 1 and ends around mid March. Some areas require removal of ice huts by March 15th. Under the general regulations for the region, the main sportfish species available for ice fishing are walleye, northern pike, trout, splake and whitefish. Be sure to check the regulations before heading out as restrictions are continually being revised on a number of lakes, especially lakes with lake trout populations.

How to Read the Depth Charts

Knowing how to read a depth chart will definitely improve your fishing success. Depth charts are the best way to find clues to where fish are hanging out. When reading depth charts there are some general rules that can help your angling success.

When analyzing a depth chart, look for hidden islands, drop-offs and shoals. A hidden island is a relatively flat, shallow area that is slightly submerged, while being surrounded by deeper water. A drop-off is a rapid decline in the depth on the chart. A shoal is a slowly declining area of the lake, which then drops off into the depths. In larger lakes, shoals can also be characterized as shallow irregularities in the bottom of the lake, essentially, a bump in the bottom. In some lakes there may be only one or two of these significant shoal sites and often is the site of some of the best angling on the lake. Shoal areas are often the site of thicker aquatic vegetation, which is home to insects and bait fish in which the larger sport fish feed on.

When looking for a species like the lake trout, depth information can be very handy. As an example, lake trout during summer often revert to the deepest part of the lake in order to find colder water for their survival. On some lakes, there may only be a specific area of the lake where lake trout will find the required depth needed for survival. With a depth chart in hand, these deep spots can be easily located.

Creek and river estuaries are always important information on any lake as fish congregate near the inflows and outflows of lakes in search of increased oxygen levels and food. At times, these areas can be the hottest spot in a lake. As an example, during the fall period, walleye will often congregate near river inflows, as a part of their migration to spawning grounds. This can be very useful information and can change the course of your angling experience on a lake or water body.

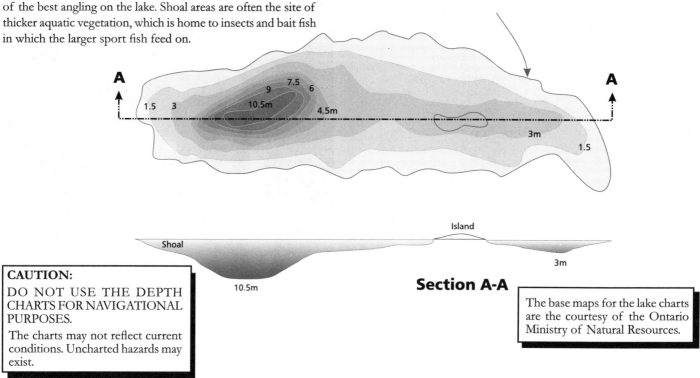

CAUTION:
DO NOT USE THE DEPTH CHARTS FOR NAVIGATIONAL PURPOSES.
The charts may not reflect current conditions. Uncharted hazards may exist.

Section A-A

The base maps for the lake charts are the courtesy of the Ontario Ministry of Natural Resources.

DEPTH CHART LEGEND

Flooded Land	Rocks	⚓ Anchorage	🚶 Hiking	FSR Forest Service Road
Indian Reserve	Sandbar	🛥 Boat Launch	Beacons	ha Hectare
Swamp / Marsh	Shoal	Lodge / Resort/ B&B	🚫 No Fishing	ac Acre
Provincial Park	Water Vegetation	● Community	P Parking	4wd 4 Wheel Drive Vehicles
		= Dam	🚻 Picnic Area	ft Feet
Highway	Side Road	Float Plane Access	★ Point of Interest	m Metres
Main Road	Old Road/Trail	5 Highway, Primary	Truck Only Campground	kg Kilogram
Stream	Lake	5A Highway, Secondary	Trail or Water Access Campsite	lbs Pounds
		Highway, Trans-Canada	Trailer and Tent Campground	Lat-N Latitude North
		Footbridge	Waterfall	Lon-W Longitude-West
		Dock/Wharf	Cabins	

Anson Lake

Access

Anson Lake is a secluded lake that lies east of the Poker Lakes and south of the Leslie M. Frost Centre. Near the north end of Kushog Lake, take the Austin Lake Road south off Highway 35. The road continuously gets rougher and requires a 4wd vehicle or ATV to traverse. There are a few branch roads, one leading to the northern shore and a cabin, the other to the eastern shore. Most anglers access this lake by snowmobile in winter.

Fishing

Anson Lake is a secluded backcountry lake that is surrounded by Crown Land. This beautiful lake is stocked every few years with the lake trout/brook trout hybrid, splake. Splake provide the best fishing opportunities during the winter through the ice. Other than the small window of opportunity at the beginning of the season, fishing for splake in the open water season is generally slow.

There are rumours that bass have made their way into Anson Lake; however, these reports have not been confirmed.

Recent Fish Stocking

Year	Fish Species	Number
2001	Splake	2,900
1999	Splake	2,900
1997	Splake	2,900

Lake Definition

Surface Area: 72 ha (180 ac)
Mean Depth: 5.9 m (19 ft)
Max Depth: 28 m (92.8 ft)
Way Point: 45° 03' 00" Lat - N
78° 54' 00" Lon - W

Facilities

Since Anson Lake is surrounded by Crown Land, rustic camping opportunities are available. Before heading into this remote lake, the village of Carnarvon and the town of Minden to the south offer all necessities needed for a great outdoor adventure.

Other Options

West of Anson Lake, visitors can access the Poker Lakes via Highway 118. The **Poker Lakes** are a series of lakes connected by portages that offer plenty of angling opportunities as well as Crown Land camping.

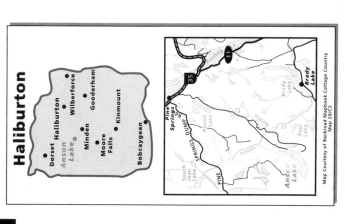

Map Courtesy of Backroad Mapbook Cottage Country
Map 26/C3

Bark Lake

Access

Access to Bark Lake is limited to a restricted access road off the north side of Highway 503. Primarily cottage owners use this road. Although a few anglers have been permitted lake access from the road in the past, this cannot be relied on.

Public access is available via a rough portage from the southeast shore of Koshlong Lake. The portage is approximately 1 km in length and accesses the north shore of Bark Lake. There are a number of public access points available on Koshlong Lake where a canoe can easily be launched into the lake.

Fishing

Bark Lake has a few cottages along its shoreline and hence the fishing pressure is low compared to many other lakes in the region. Regardless of this limited angling pressure, fishing in the lake is regarded as fair for decent sized smallmouth bass. Bass average around 0.5 kg (1 lb) although much larger bass are caught in the lake annually.

The two hot spots on the lake are the southernmost bay and along the two underwater points located in the eastern portion of the lake. The southern bay is home to plenty of underwater rock structure providing ideal habitat and cover for bass. Try working a tube jig or streamer type fly along this structure to entice aggressive bass into striking. The underwater point area in the east is also a fair holding area, although a more subtle presentation is often required for success.

Throughout the lake, tube jigs are often productive, while a crayfish type fly stripped along bottom structure is always a good tactic for smallmouth. Other than bass, panfish in the lake such as perch can provide plenty of action throughout the season.

Other Options

Lost Lake is a secluded water body that is located southeast of Bark Lake. The lake is accessible by rough trail or portage from Bark Lake or from the Bark Lake cottage access road. Fishing in Lost Lake is regarded as better than in Bark Lake. Decent sized smallmouth bass can be caught in the smaller lake by using jigs and flies.

Lake Definition

Elevation:	343 m (1,143 ft)
Surface Area:	168 ha (420 ac)
Mean Depth:	4.6 m (15 ft)
Max Depth:	12.2 m (40 ft)
Way Point:	44° 56' 00" Lat - N
	78° 28' 00" Lon - W

Facilities

There are no publicly accessible facilities available on Bark Lake.

Haliburton

- Dorset Haliburton
- Wilberforce
- Minden Bark Lake
- Gooderham
- Moore Falls
- Kinmount
- Bobcaygeon

To Lost Lake

N

To Highway 503

Bark Creek

9m
12
6
3m
3m
3m
6

Scale

200m 0 200m 400m 600m 800m 1000m

Barnum Lake

Access

Located due south from the town of Haliburton, Barnum Lake can be accessed by canoe or car top boat from the east side of County Road 1. The lake is also accessible by the Victoria Rail Trail that traverses along the eastern shore of the lake.

Facilities

While there are no facilities at Barnum Lake, the town of Haliburton is minutes away to the north and has plenty to offer visitors including accommodations, restaurants and retailers. Alternatively, the Victoria Rail Trail that leads past the eastern shore of Barnum Lake is a popular long distance trail for visitors to explore.

Fishing

Most anglers would simply drive right by this small roadside lake assuming the lake is heavily fished and devoid of any sportfish. Contrary to this opinion, Barnum Lake offers fair fishing that can be good periodically for both smallmouth and largemouth bass. Since the lake is quite weedy, largemouth bass are the predominant species found in the lake.

Shoreline structure holds a number of average sized bass in the 0.5-1 kg (1-2 lb) range. Structure that is often overlooked is boat and dock areas near the cottages located along the western shore. Fly anglers can have a lot of fun casting top water poppers in these areas, while spincasters should try smaller top water presentations. A floating minnow imitation lure can also work surprisingly well along the weed lines of this lake.

Other Options

There are numerous lakes in the nearby area for anglers to test. The closest options are **Grass Lake** and **Head Lake**, which are both found to the north. Grass Lake is attached to the much larger Kashagawigamog Lake and provides fishing opportunities for bass, walleye and the odd muskellunge. Head Lake, which is closer to Haliburton, is accessible off Highway 121 and is inhabited with smallmouth bass and the odd muskellunge.

Lake Definition

Elevation: 317 m (1,057 ft)
Surface Area: 32 ha (80 ac)
Mean Depth: 3.1 m (10.5 ft)
Max Depth: 10 m (33 ft)
Perimeter: 2 km (1 mi)
Way Point: 45° 02' 00" Lat - N
78° 32' 00" Lon - W

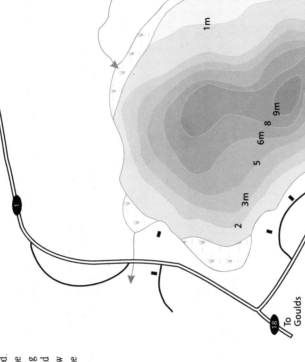

Barnum Lake

To Haliburton

Victoria Rail Trail

Barnum Creek

To Donald

To Goulds

N

Scale

100m   0   100m   200m   300m

Haliburton

Dorset Haliburton
Minden Wilberforce
Gooderham
Moore Falls Kinmount
Bobcaygeon

Haliburton
Head Lake
Barnum Lake
Grass Lake
To Soyers Lake
To Donald

Map Courtesy of Backroad Mapbook Cottage Country
Map 27/E4

Basshaunt Lake

Access

To reach Basshaunt Lake, follow Highway 118 to Eagle Lake Road (County Road 14). Follow this road north to the settlement of Eagle Lake and the junction with North Road. Take North Road east to Deer Lake Road, which travels southeast to the boat launch along the northwest end of Basshaunt Lake.

Fishing

Basshaunt Lake was being stocked regularly with lake trout in the 1990's, although over the years this process has been phased out. The stocking program was initially done to supplement existing natural stocks, but the lake should be able to sustain its lake trout population in the future. Regulations such as a fish sanctuary for the winter/spring period to aid lake trout in surviving the winter and early spring periods have been imposed to help aid the species. If you do plan to fish for lakers in Basshaunt Lake, please consider practicing catch and release, as the species is very fragile.

The other main sportfish available in Basshaunt Lake is smallmouth bass. Fishing success for smallmouth bass is fair to good at times for smallmouth that can exceed 1.5 kg (3.5 lbs) in size on occasion. Work shoreline structure with deep probing lures and flies to locate ambush ready smallmouth. Manmade shore structure should not be ruled out. Try casting along docks and boathouses for hiding bass.

Other Options

Two lakes that offer fishing opportunities in the area are **Bushwolf Lake** to the south and **West Lake** to the north. Both lakes are inhabited by populations of smallmouth bass, while West Lake is stocked regularly with rainbow trout. Both lakes are accessible by 2wd roads and have a few cottages along their shorelines.

Facilities

There is a boat launch and several cottages around Basshaunt Lake, while Camp Kakeka is found along the southern shore. People looking for a more luxurious vacation can try the nearby Sir Sam's Inn. It is a popular year round vacationing retreat that is found west of the lake.

Lake Definition

Mean Depth: 12 m (39.4 ft)
Max Depth: 21 m (70 ft)
Way Point: 45° 07' 00" Lat - N
78° 28' 00" Lon - W

Recent Fish Stocking

Year	Fish Species
1998	Lake Trout
1997	Lake Trout
1996	Lake Trout

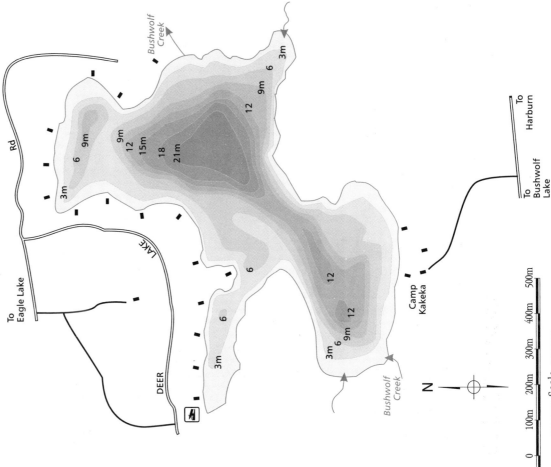

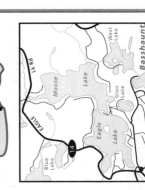

Haliburton

Map Courtesy of Backroad Mapbook Cottage Country
Map 27/F1

Big Hawk Lake

Access

This large lake lies within the Leslie M. Frost Centre, although there are cottages located along much of the lake's shoreline. Big Hawk Lake Road provides access to a boat launch along the southwestern shore of the lake. While the boat launch is the most popular access to the lake, the lake can also be reached by water or portage from a number of nearby Frost Centre lakes.

Fishing

Smallmouth bass are the most abundant sportfish found in Big Hawk Lake, and there have been reports that largemouth bass also inhabit the lake. Fishing for bass is slow to fair at times for bass that average 0.5-1 kg (1-2 lbs) in size.

The rocky shoreline of the lake provides good cover for smallmouth. One area in particular that tends to hold numbers of smallmouth is off the west side of the large island found in the middle of the lake. For success, try working darker coloured jigs or streamers along these rocky shoreline areas. Crayfish imitation lures and flies can also work well on this lake. Present the lure or fly close to bottom structure and retrieve in short quick strips, imitating a fleeing crayfish.

It is rumoured that brook trout once inhabited Big Hawk Lake, but there have been no recent reports on this popular sportfish species. Instead, anglers will be happy to know there is a natural population of lake trout in the big lake. Unfortunately, the numbers are low and fishing success is often slow. Trolling in the early part of the season is the most effective way in finding lake trout. If you do fish for these trout, please practice catch and release and watch for special restrictions on lake trout.

Facilities

The **Leslie M. Frost Centre** is used as a training centre for Ontario Ministry of Natural Resources staff, and is a popular outdoor recreation destination for locals. The centre property spans well past Big Hawk Lake and contains numerous secluded lakes that can be accessed by trail, road or portage. Free Crown Land campsites have been established along most lakes in the centre and can be quite busy during the months of July and August. For more information please contact the centre at (705) 766-2451 or visit their website at www.frostcentre.on.ca

Other Options

While there are a few portage access lakes close to Big Hawk Lake, **Little Hawk Lake** and **Nunikani Lake** are two of the easiest lakes that can be reached by water from Big Hawk Lake. Little Hawk Lake lies to the south of Big Hawk Lake while Nunikani Lake is located to the north. Both lakes are inhabited by lake trout and smallmouth bass providing spring to fall angling opportunities

Lake Definition

Elevation:	354 m (1,180 ft)
Surface Area:	39 ha (98 ac)
Mean Depth:	16.4 m (54.8 ft)
Max Depth:	54 m (180 ft)
Perimeter:	16 km (10 mi)
Way Point:	45° 10' 00" Lat - N
	78° 44' 00" Lon - W

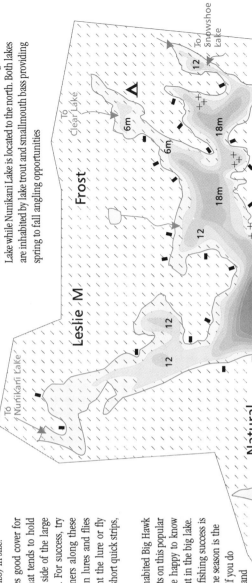

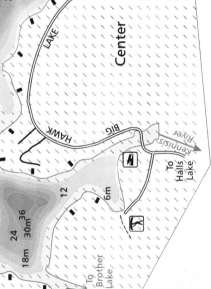

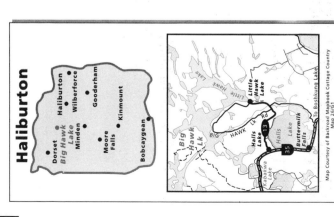

Haliburton

Dorset
Big Hawk Lake
Haliburton
Minden
Wilberforce
Gooderham
Moore Falls
Kinmount
Bobcaygeon

Map Courtesy of Backroad Mapbook Cottage Country Map 26/G1

· Billings Lake

Access

To find Billings Lake, follow County Road 503 east of Gooderham to the Wolf Lake Road. Wolf Lake Road travels north to the Billings Lake Dam located along the southern shore of the lake. At the dam area, a small boat launch is available.

Other Options

To the southwest of Billings Lake, **Gooderham Lake** is a decent smallmouth bass and walleye angling alternative. Also in the area is a small lake named **Little Bob Lake** that has been stocked regularly with brook trout.

Fishing

There are many cottages along the shoreline of Billings Lake but that doesn't seem to affect the fishing for smallmouth bass. Smallmouth are present in fair to good numbers but the feisty fish are generally small, averaging about 1 kg (2 lbs) in size. Walleye are also present in this lake; however, fishing success is generally limited.

Smallmouth can be found nearby all of the islands found on the lake and also frequent man-made structure areas such as boat docks. In particular, the small island found in the eastern end of the lake is a decent holding area. There is also plenty of weed structure in the lake to provide habitat for baitfish, which attract both walleye and bass. Casting jigs along this type of shore structure can produce surprising results for both species. Top water poppers and flies can be a lot of fun in the shallower areas of the lake for aggressive bass.

Facilities

Being a cottage destination lake, public facilities are limited to the boat launch at the south end of the lake near the dam.

Lake Definition

Elevation:	354 m (1,143 ft)
Surface Area:	10 ha (25 ac)
Mean Depth:	6.1 m (20.6 ft)
Max Depth:	37.2 m (124 ft)
Perimeter:	7 km (4 mi)
Way Point:	44° 56' 00" Lat - N
	78° 22' 00" Lon - W

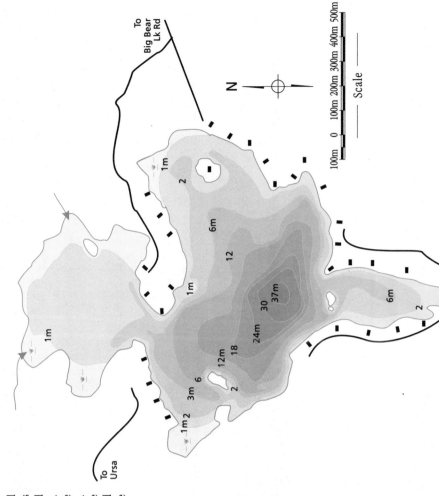

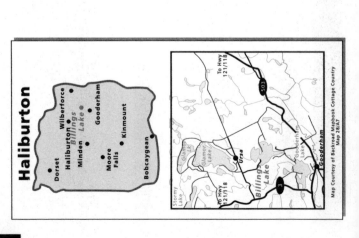

Map Courtesy of Backroad Mapbook Cottage Country Map 28/A7

Black Lake

Access

This small lake lies just off Highway 121 east of the town of Haliburton. Access roads branch from the highway leading along the north, south and eastern shoreline. A boat launch is available along the southeast shore of the lake.

Other Options

Haas Lake lies to the west of Black Lake off the south side of Highway 121, while **Blue Hawk Lake** is located south along Buckhorn Road. Both lakes are home to populations of walleye, smallmouth bass and the odd muskellunge. Success in both lakes is best for smallmouth bass.

Fishing

Rainbow trout were stocked in Black Lake several years ago, but the lake is not suitable for rainbow trout to thrive. All rainbow trout are now gone and the natural sportfish, smallmouth bass, are the focus of anglers. Fishing pressure on the lake is regarded as moderate to heavy, due to the close proximity of Highway 121.

Due to the fishing pressure, angling success is slow to fair for smallmouth that average around 0.5 kg (1 lb) in size. There is plenty of weed growth on the lake during the season and bass normally hang out along weed lines. Try working a jig through weed areas or a top water lure or fly during evening or overcast periods.

Facilities

A boat launch provides anglers access to the lake. The nearby town of Haliburton has plenty to offer area visitors such as accommodations, fishing retailers and restaurants.

Lake Definition

Elevation:	360 m (1,200 ft)
Surface Area:	24 ha (60 ac)
Mean Depth:	3.1 m (10.5 ft)
Max Depth:	8.4 m (28 ft)
Perimeter:	3 km (1.9 mi)
Way Point:	45° 03' 00" Lat - N
	78° 25' 00" Lon - W

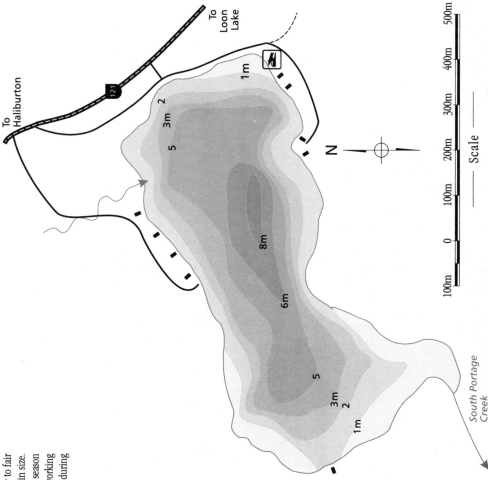

Black Lake

To Haliburton

To Loon Lake

121

1m
2
3m
5
8m
6m
5
3m
2
1m

N

South Portage Creek

Scale

100m   0   100m   200m   300m   400m   500m

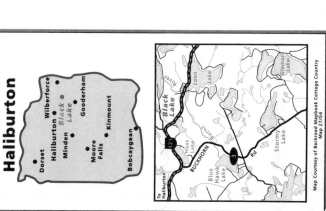

Haliburton

Dorset
Wilberforce
Haliburton
Minden
Black Lake
Gooderham
Moore Falls
Kinmount
Bobcaygean

Black Lake
Loon Lake
Glamot Lake
RIVER
Burn
Haas Lake
BUCKHORN
Blue Hawk Lake
Stormy Lake
Rd
To Haliburton
121

Map Courtesy of Backroad Mapbook Cottage Country Map 27/G4

Black (Eyre) Lake

Access

This Black Lake lies within the Haliburton Forest Reserve. To reach the lake, follow the Kennisis Lake Road (County Road 7) north to the Forest Reserve front gate. From the front gate, Black Lake can be found by following the East Road. Black Lake lies to the east of Clean Lake.

Facilities

Camping opportunities exist at Black Lake. Permits can be purchased at the main gatehouse of the Haliburton Forest Reserve. For visitors looking for more elaborate accommodations, the reserve does have a number of cottages for rent as well as rooms in the main lodge. A small general store is also available in the reserve. For more information on the Haliburton Forest Reserve, check out www.haliburtonforest.com.

Fishing

Black Lake is a unique lake due to the fact that the natural lake trout that inhabit the lake are a unique strain that is only found in nearby Clean Lake and MacDonald Lake. While these Haliburton forest lake trout are usually smaller than most other Ontario lake trout, they seem to be more numerous. Fishing for these lakers is fair for lake trout to 40 cm (16 in) in size. Ice fishing is popular on this lake and success is consistent through the ice and in the early portion of the open water season.

Over the years, both smallmouth and largemouth bass have found their way into the lake and have established a naturally reproducing population. Fishing for bass is good at times for bass that average around 0.5-1 kg (1-2 lbs) in size. Try flipping jigs and spinners along shore structure for aggressive bass.

Please practice catch and release in order to help maintain the unique lake trout and bass species in Black Lake.

Other Options

Little Black Lake is connected by stream to Black Lake and offers similar fishing opportunities. Little Black is also inhabited with a natural strain of lake trout, as well as smallmouth and largemouth bass.

Lake Definition

Surface Area:	71 ha (178 ac)
Mean Depth:	7.6 m (25 ft)
Max Depth:	17.3 m (57 ft)
Way Point:	45° 15' 00" Lat - N
	78° 30' 00" Lon - W

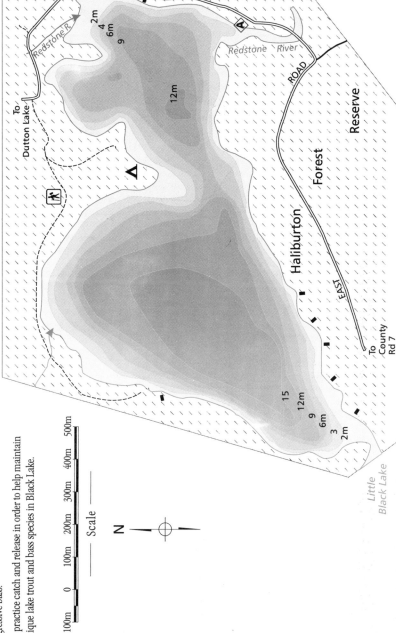

Blue Lake

Access

North of Haliburton, Blue Lake is accessible off the Eagle Lake Road (County Road 14). The Eagle Lake Road can be picked up off the north side of Highway 118, west of Haliburton.

Lake Definition

Surface Area: 21 ha (53 ac)
Mean Depth: 2.7 m (9 ft)
Max Depth: 9.7 m (32 ft)
Way Point: 45° 09' 00" Lat - N
78° 30' 00" Lon - W

Fishing

This smaller sized lake has a few cottages along its shoreline and is stocked every few years with splake. Fishing for splake is best during the winter through the ice or in the spring just after ice off. In the winter, anglers should try jigging small spoons about 3-5 m (10-16 ft) below the surface and along shallower shoal areas of the lake. Splake are not overly large in Blue Lake and average around 30-40 cm (12-16 in) in size.

In the summer months, fishing in Blue Lake is best for its resident smallmouth bass. Success for bass is generally fair for bass that average 0.5 kg (1 lb) in size. All the normal smallmouth tactics work well. For something a little different, fly anglers should try stripping in Wooly Buggers or minnow imitation flies to entice smallmouth hits.

Facilities

There are no facilities available at Blue Lake; however, the nearby town of Haliburton has plenty to offer. Visitors will find accommodations, groceries and numerous other retail operations.

Other Options

To the south of Blue Lake lies **Pot Lake** and **Frying Pan Lake**. These two small lakes are somewhat secluded and offer fishing for smallmouth bass. Eagle Lake Road travels past the eastern shore of Pot Lake, while Frying Pan Lake can be accessed via a short portage from Pot Lake.

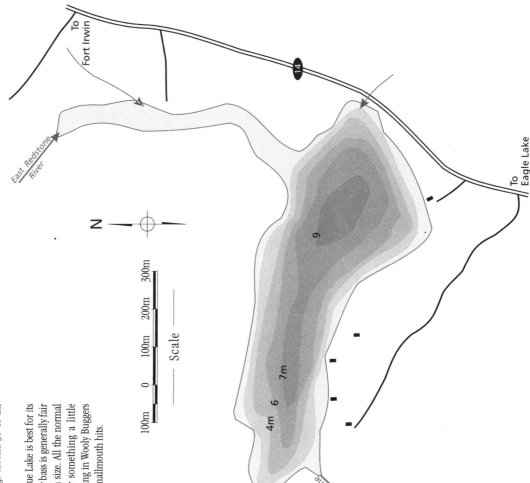

East Redstone River

To Fort Irwin

14

To Eagle Lake

East Redstone River

4m 6 7m 9

N

100m 0 100m 200m 300m
— Scale —

Haliburton

Dorset
Blue Lake
Haliburton
Wilberforce
Minden
Gooderham
Moore Falls
Kinmount
Bobcaygeon

Map Courtesy of Backroad Mapbook Cottage Country Map 27/E1

To Haliburton Lake
Lk Rd
West Lake
Moose Lake
Glen Lake
Basshaunt Lake
EAGLE
Eagle Lake
Blue Lake
14
Eagle To Lake
Hwy 118

Blue Hawk Lake

Access

This small lake can be reached within a few minutes from the town of Haliburton. From Haliburton, take Highway 121 east to Buckhorn Road (County Road 3). Buckhorn Road heads south past the eastern shore of Blue Hawk Lake and a small boat launch area.

Other Options

If the action on Blue Hawk Lake is too slow, **Stormy Lake** is a decent alternative. South of Blue Hawk Lake, Stormy Lake lies off the east side of Buckhorn Road and offers fishing opportunities for lake trout and smallmouth bass. Watch for special regulations on this lake.

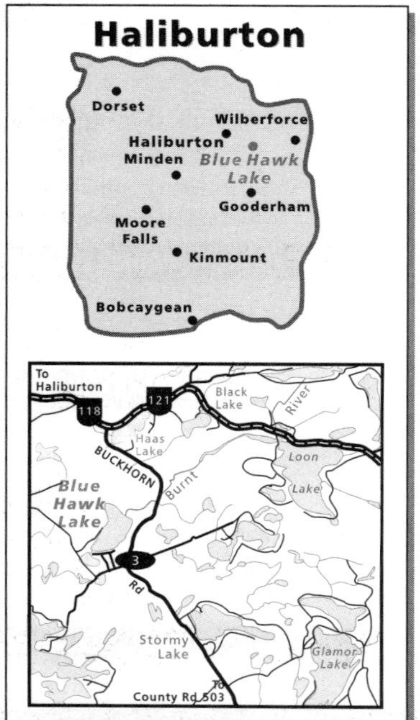

Fishing

Blue Hawk Lake is a dark coloured lake that hosts plenty of aquatic vegetation. The lake can be busy at times during the summer months; however, it continues to produce decent angling results. Anglers can expect to find fair to good fishing at times for smallmouth and largemouth bass and slow to fair fishing for resident walleye. A small population of muskellunge also exists in Blue Hawk Lake.

Bass frequent the many weedy areas found around the lake and also hang around the 3 m (10 ft) shoal located along the southeastern end of the lake. While subsurface flies and lures are the most consistent attractant for bass, top water action can heat up on this lake at times. Try top water techniques in the evening or during overcast periods.

Walleye and muskellunge are often hard to find in Blue Hawk Lake. Some of the more popular angling methods for walleye are trolling a worm harness or a minnow imitation lure as well as still jigging with various coloured and scented jigs. Fishing for musky is inconsistent throughout the summer months, although during the fall musky are often caught in shallow areas, mainly along weed lines.

Facilities

Visitors to Blue Hawk Lake can access the lake from the public boat launch area found just off the west side of Buckhorn Road (County Road 3). Supplies and all necessities can be found in the nearby town of Haliburton.

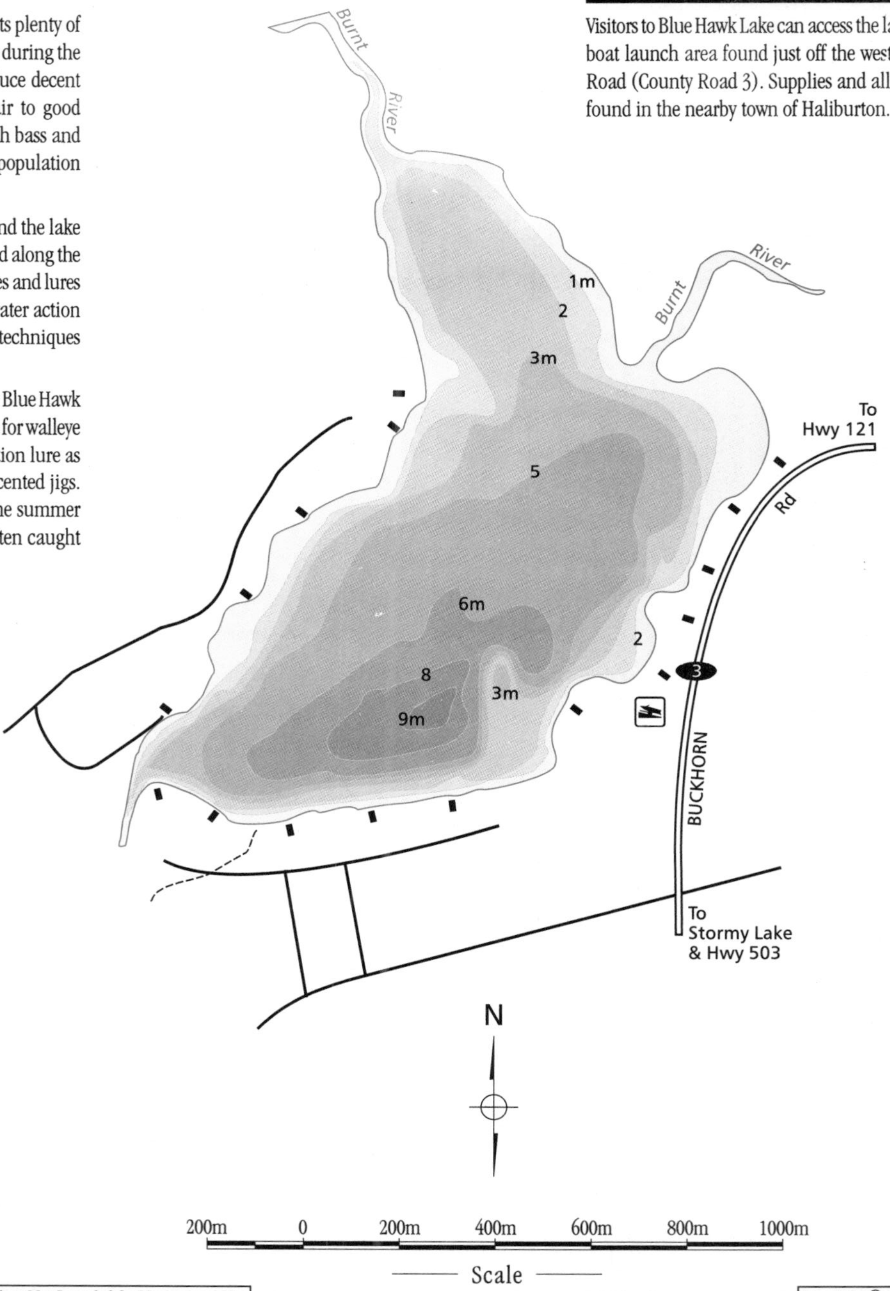

Lake Definition

Elevation: 351 m (1,152 ft)
Surface Area: 74 ha (185 ac)
Mean Depth: 4.5 m (15 ft)
Max Depth: 9 m (29.5 ft)
Perimeter: 4 km (3 mi)
Way Point: 45° 00' 00" Lat - N
78° 27' 00" Lon - W

Map Courtesy of Backroad Mapbook Cottage Country
Map 27/F5

Bob Lake

Access

This popular cottage destination lake is found just west of the town of Minden. From Minden, follow County Road 2 west to Big Bob Lake Road. Big Bob Lake Road leads along the west side of the lake, passing by a public boat launch at the southern end of the lake.

Other Options

Beer Lake and **Swamp Lake** are located north and west respectively of Bob Lake and offer fishing opportunities for smallmouth and largemouth bass. Beer Lake is accessible by a 2wd vehicle, while a high clearance 4wd truck would be required to reach Swamp Lake.

Fishing

Bob Lake is part of the headwater system for the Trent Canal and there is a water level regulating dam at the southern most point on the lake. Due to the dam, water levels on the lake can fluctuate up to 3 m (10 ft) affecting fishing success at times.

The rocky shoreline of Bob Lake provides good habitat for its resident smallmouth bass. There are also rumours that largemouth are now present in the lake. Smallmouth average about 0.5 kg (1 lb) in size, although can be caught up to 2 kg (4.5 lbs) in size on occasion. Success for bass is regarded as fair and is best during overcast or evening periods. Bass are often caught off any of the rocky islands found around the lake. The key to success is to locate underwater rock structure and work the bottom areas with your lure or fly.

The deep cool nature of the lake creates ideal habitat for a natural population of lake trout. The lake was once quite good for lake trout fishing; however, the combination of water level fluctuations and increased fishing pressure over the years has reduced success to slow to fair. Ice fishing is quite popular for lake trout in this lake and perhaps the most effective way to catch them. Jigging a small silver spoon off shoal areas can be productive. Slot size restrictions and the fact that many anglers are practicing catch and release for natural stocks should help improve this fishery in the coming years.

Facilities

The town of Minden is located minutes east of Bob Lake and is home to a number of retailers, restaurants and other amenities. A Ministry of Natural Resources office is also located in town.

Lake Definition

Elevation:	292 m (973 ft)
Surface Area:	220 ha (550 ac)
Mean Depth:	17.8 m (59.5 ft)
Max Depth:	63 m (210 ft)
Perimeter:	15.6 km (9.8 mi)
Way Point:	44° 55' 00" Lat - N
	78° 47' 00" Lon - W

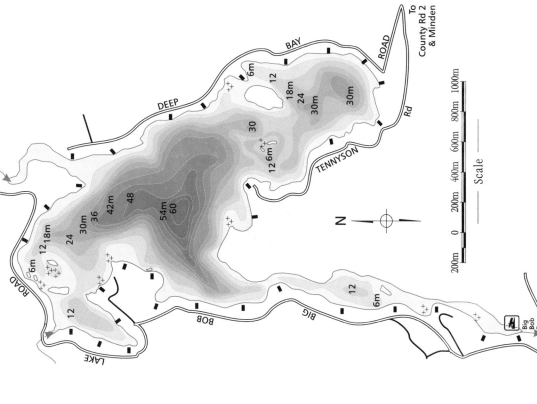

To County Rd 2 & Minden

To Hwy 35

Scale

200m 0 200m 400m 600m 800m 1000m

N

Big Bob Dam

Haliburton

Dorset · Haliburton · Wilberforce
Minden · Gooderham
Moore Falls · Kinmount
Bobcaygeon
Bob Lake

Map Courtesy of Backroad Mapbook Cottage Country Map 26/F7

Boshkung Lake

Access

Boshkung Lake is located just outside of the village of Carnarvon. Highway 35 travels along the eastern shore of the lake and a canoe can be launched in a few spots from the highway, although it is not recommended. Boat access is available from one of the privately organized lodges or resorts on the lake.

Other Options

North of Boshkung Lake, **Saskatchewan Lake** can be found just off Highway 35. Saskatchewan Lake is a small Leslie M. Frost Centre lake that offers fishing opportunities for both smallmouth and largemouth bass.

Fishing

The close proximity of Boshkung Lake to Highway 35 makes it a popular destination, especially in the summer. This has affected the lake trout fishery somewhat but smallmouth and largemouth bass seem unaffected by the number of anglers.

Bass can be found up to the 1.5 kg (3.5 lb) range, although they average around 0.5-1 kg (1-2 lbs). Look for bass off rock drop-offs or around weed structure. The inflow from Halls Lake and Beech Lake can be productive areas for bass.

The natural population of lake trout seems to disappear at times in this deep lake. (Boshkung Lake has an average depth of 23 m/76 ft and a maximum depth of 70 m/229 ft). This makes finding lake trout rather difficult during the heat of the summer. For this reason, the fish are more often targeted during the winter ice fishing season. Anglers do not have to fish as deep and can jig though the ice with small spoons and various other lures. A few of the more productive ice fishing locations are located off any of the points found along the lake. In order to maintain the natural lake trout fishery, slot size and special ice fishing regulations have been established.

Facilities

Buttermilk Falls Resort provides all amenities including: self-catering cottages, docks, fireplaces, safe sandy beach, playground and horseshoe pits. Located right beside Buttermilk Falls, the resort is open all year and offers canoe and rowboat rentals as well as ice fishing huts in the winter. For more information or reservations call 1-888-368-3147 or visit www.buttermilkfallsresort.com.

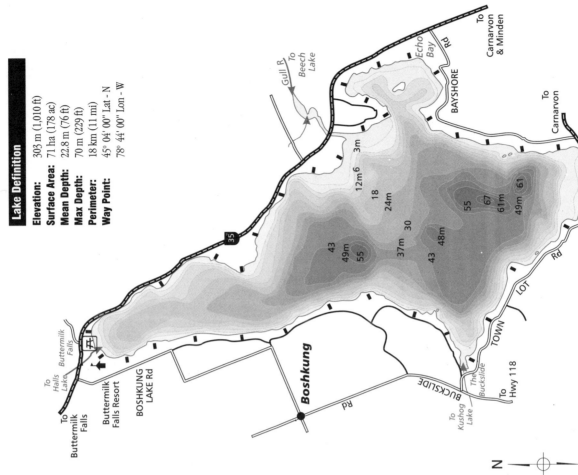

Lake Definition

Elevation:	303 m (1,010 ft)
Surface Area:	71 ha (178 ac)
Mean Depth:	22.8 m (76 ft)
Max Depth:	70 m (229 ft)
Perimeter:	18 km (11 mi)
Way Point:	45° 04' 00" Lat - N
	78° 44' 00" Lon - W

Scale

400m 0 400m 800m 1200m 1600m

Haliburton

Dorset Haliburton
Wilberforce
Minden Gooderham
Moore Kinmount
Falls
Bobcaygeon

Map Courtesy of Backroad Mapbook Cottage Country
Map 26/G3

Brady Lake

Access

Brady Lake is a long, somewhat narrow lake that lays not far off Highway 118 west of the village of Carnarvon. From Carnarvon, follow Highway 118 west to the Brady Lake Road. Brady Lake Road leads along the southern shore of Brady Lake and passes a roadside access point. The access is best suited for cartop boats and canoes.

Fishing

Brady Lake is a generally shallow lake with an average depth of 4 m (14 ft). The lake provides good habitat for its resident bass population with plenty of weed structure throughout. Fishing for both smallmouth and largemouth is regarded as fair to good at times. Bass can be found in the 1.5 kg (3.5 lb) range and top water poppers can be a lot of fun on this lake, especially during overcast periods. However, the bass are moody and there are times when success for bass can be quite frustrating.

Rainbow trout were unsuccessfully stocked in Brady Lake in the distant past. Today, no trout are found but there is a small population of muskellunge. Success is usually slow but determined hunters have been known to find the odd musky.

Other Options

Paul Lake is located west of Brady Lake and is accessible via a rough 4wd road. The secluded lake provides angling opportunities for both smallmouth and largemouth bass. Further west is the **Poker Lake Chain**. A popular canoe route has been established here and it connects several lakes. The bass fishing is excellent and the wilderness camping sites make the perfect getaway.

Facilities

Small boats and canoes can be launched at lakeside near the community of Brady Lake. No other facilities are offered at the lake.

Lake Definition

Elevation: 295 m (983 ft)
Surface Area: 66 ha (165 ac)
Mean Depth: 4.2 m (14 ft)
Max Depth: 10.5 m (35 ft)
Perimeter: 10 km (6 mi)
Way Point: 45° 05' 00" Lat - N
78° 50' 00" Lon - W

Haliburton

Map Courtesy of Backroad Mapbook Cottage Country Map 26/E4

Depth Chart Not Intended for Navigational Use

Haliburton

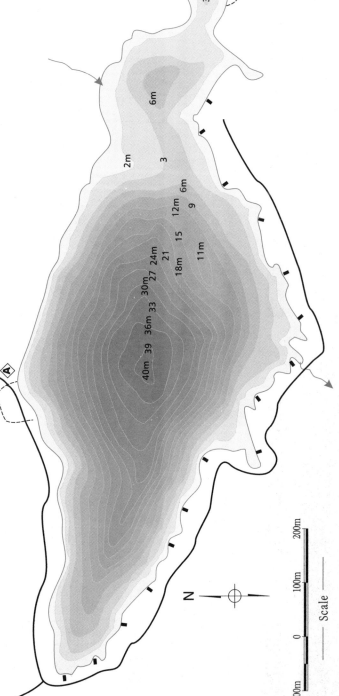

Map Courtesy of Backroad Mapbook Cottage Country
Map 28/E6

Buckskin Lake

Access

Visitors can find this secluded lake east of the village of Tory Hill. From Tory Hill, follow Highway 121 east to the Rock Lake Road. The gravel road treks south to a rough car top/canoe access point on the northern shore of the lake.

Lake Definition

Surface Area: 32 ha (80 ac)
Mean Depth: 20.3 m (66.8 ft)
Max Depth: 40 m (132 ft)
Way Point: 44° 57' 00" Lat - N
78° 11' 00" Lon - W

Fishing

Buckskin Lake has been stocked over the years with splake, rainbow trout and lake trout. Most recently, the lake has been stocked annually with lake trout and was on a semi-annually stocking program for rainbow trout until 1999. Rainbow trout success has slowed considerably in recent years and it is unknown whether the stocking of rainbows will occur in the future. Success for lakers is regarded as fair to good at times, although fishing is best through the ice in winter. After spring, lakers revert to the depths of this deep lake and are considerably more difficult to catch.

The best bet for fishing success on Buckskin Lake is for its resident smallmouth bass. Bass fishing is fair to good at times that average around 1 kg (2 lbs) in size. Smallmouth are best found along shore areas along rocky drop-offs. Try working a crayfish or leech pattern along shore structure for ambush ready smallmouth. Crankbaits and jigs can also be quite effective.

Other Options

The access road to Buckskin Lake also passes by **Monrock Lake.** Monrock Lake offers similar fishing opportunities for smallmouth bass as Buckskin Lake. Many regard Monrock Lake as a better bass lake than Buckskin Lake. Additionally, **Adams Lake** to the east is accessible just off Highway 121. This lake is stocked periodically with brook trout.

Facilities

Other than the rustic launching area, there are no facilities available at Buckskin Lake.

Recent Fish Stocking

Year	Fish Species	Number
2002	Lake trout	300
2001	Lake trout	300
2001	Splake	1,300
2000	Lake trout	300

Burdock Lake

Access

To reach Burdock Lake, follow Highway 118 west from Haliburton to the Kennisis Lake Road (County Road 7). The Kennisis Lake Road travels north, eventually passing by the western end of Burdock Lake.

Lake Definition

Surface Area: 15 ha (38 ac)
Mean Depth: 4.3 m (14 ft)
Max Depth: 10.6 m (35 ft)
Way Point: 45° 10' 00" Lat - N
78° 35' 00" Lon - W

Fishing

This small lake is heavily stocked with brook trout. As a result, fishing for brookies can be good at times, especially in the winter or in the spring, just after ice off. Ice fishing is most productive along shoreline areas. Try jigging a small spoon or light coloured jig in 3-5 m (10-16 ft) of water. Brookies usually cruise closer to the surface where oxygen levels are at their best. In the spring, spincasting or trolling small spoons or spinners can be productive. Fly anglers should try a Muddler Minnow or small nymph pattern.

Live fish are not permitted for use as bait in this lake.

Other Options

En route to Burdock Lake, the Kennisis Lake Road passes between **Silver Lake** and **Centre Lake**. Silver Lake offers fishing opportunities for smallmouth bass, while Centre Lake is rumoured to still support a natural brook trout fishery. The small lake has also been stocked with splake in the past.

Facilities

There are no facilities available at Burdock Lake. For camping and other overnight accommodations, the Haliburton Forest Reserve is located north of the lake. Alternatively, the town of Haliburton to the south has plenty to offer visitors.

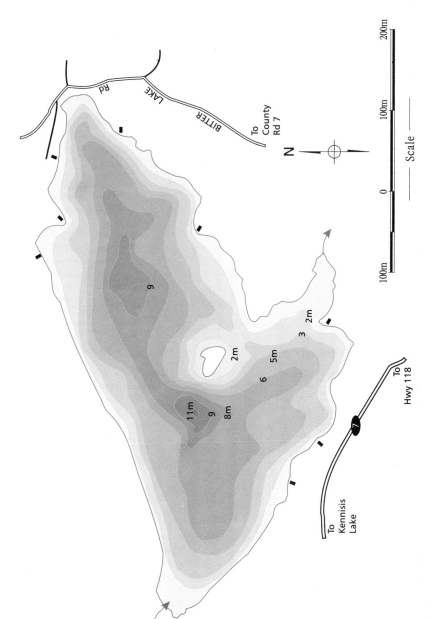

Copyright © Mussio Ventures Ltd.

Depth Chart Not Intended for Navigational Use

23

Canning Lake

Access

Canning Lake is located northeast of the town of Minden. To find the lake, follow Highway 35 north from Minden to Highway 121 and head east. There are several access roads that branch south off Highway 121, including County Road 17, towards Canning Lake.

Facilities

There are no public facilities available on Canning Lake, although private cottages may be available for rent. Check the local real estate agencies for rental information.

Fishing

This popular cottage destination lake is probably better known for its recreation opportunities rather than its fishing. Bass fishing can be fair to good at times for smallmouth and largemouth bass up to 1.5 kg (3.5 lbs) in size. Other species present in Canning Lake include walleye, lake trout and muskellunge. Fishing success for these three species is generally limited.

There is plenty of shore structure around the lake for bass to hide in as well as a fantastic shoal area in the eastern end of the lake. The shoal is a favourite holding area for bass and is best worked with a tube jig or streamer type fly.

Other Options

For outdoor recreation enthusiasts, the **Drag/Burnt River Canoe Route** can be accessed from the Canning Lake Dam, which is located along the southeast shore of the lake. The canoe route can be followed south all the way to the junction with the Irondale River and eventually past the town of Kinmount. Bass and other warm water species are prevalent in these river systems.

Lake Definition

Elevation:	286 m (953 ft)
Surface Area:	196 ha (490 ac)
Mean Depth:	6m (20 ft)
Max Depth:	20.1m (67 ft)
Perimeter:	16km (10 mi)
Way Point:	44° 56' 00" Lat - N
	78° 38' 00" Lon - W

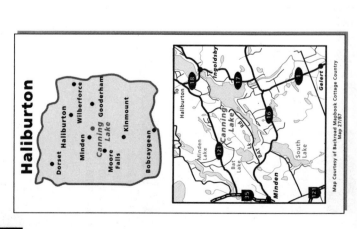

Map Courtesy of Backroad Mapbook Cottage Country Map 27/B7

Clean (Clear) Lake

Access

Whether it is called Clean or Clear, this lake lies off East Road within the Haliburton Forest Reserve. The Haliburton Forest Reserve is a private recreation area that permits public access for a fee. The reserve can be reached by following the Kennisis Lake Road (County Road 7) north from Highway 118.

Other Options

MacDonald Lake and **Black Lake** lie to the west and east of Clean Lake respectively. The unique strain of Haliburton lake trout is found in each lake as well as smallmouth and largemouth bass.

Fishing

Clean Lake is part of a chain of three lakes that are inhabited by a unique strain of lake trout. The strain is indigenous to the Haliburton Forest and is characteristically smaller than most other Ontario lake trout. However, this strain makes up for their generally smaller size by being more abundant. There are also smallmouth and largemouth bass in the lake.

During the open water season, trolling is the best method to catch lake trout. Anglers will also find that just after ice off, lakers can be caught near the surface on flies as well as lures and spinners. Ice fishing is usually the most effective time to catch lake trout. Jigging a small spoon or even white jigs through the ice in the 3 m (10 ft) depth range can stir up some good action.

During the summer, angling attention turns to bass. Success for both smallmouth and largemouth bass can be good for fish that average about 0.5-1 kg (1-2 lbs) in size. Typical methods for bass can be effective in Clean Lake such as shore casting with spinner baits and jigs.

Be sure to check the regulations before heading out. There are special season regulations on this lake.

Facilities

The Haliburton Forest is a privately owned recreation paradise that offers a variety of outdoor recreation opportunities including camping, backcountry exploration and of course, fishing. Full modern accommodations are offered at the reserve including a full service lodge or individual housekeeping units. Along with the many angling opportunities available in the reserve, visitors can explore over 300 km (186 mi) of backcountry roads and trails. The forest reserve also offers a variety of outdoor educational programs to enhance your wilderness skills and knowledge. For more information call (705) 754-2198 or visit www.haliburtonforest.com

Lake Definition

Elevation:	375 m (1,250 ft)
Surface Area:	160 ha (400 ac)
Mean Depth:	14.5 m (48.6 ft)
Max Depth:	42.6 m (142 ft)
Perimeter:	6.7 km (4.2 mi)
Way Point:	45° 15' 00" Lat - N
	78° 32' 00" Lon - W

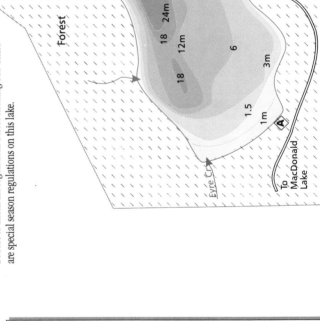

Map Courtesy of Backroad Mapbook Cottage Country Map 34/E6

Clement Lake

Access

Clement Lake lies near the settlement of Wilberforce, east of Haliburton. To reach the lake, follow Highway 121 to Highway 648 and head north. At the junction with the Burleigh Road (County Road 15), take the Burleigh Road northwest. The Burleigh Road soon passes by the northern shore of the lake and the public boat launch area.

Facilities

The public boat launch area is the main public facility available at Clement Lake.

Fishing

Rainbow trout were regularly stocked in Clement Lake over the years. However, the last time the lake was stocked was as far back as 1999 and trout fishing has been marginal over the last few years. It is unclear whether or not the lake will be stocked again in the future.

Smallmouth bass are also present in Clement Lake. They provide for fair to good fishing at times for bass that average around 1 kg (2 lbs) in size. The clear nature of the lake can create spooky bass, especially on bright days. Subtle tactics like using a dark coloured lure or fly can increase results. For fly casters try a dark leech pattern or crayfish imitation, while spincasters often have decent results with tube jigs.

Other Options

North of Clement Lake, **Yankton Lake** can be accessed via a 4wd road from County Road 15. The lake also holds a natural population of smallmouth bass and was once stocked with rainbow trout. Since fewer people visit the lake, fishing success can be better than in Clement.

Lake Definition

Elevation:	384 m (1,280 ft)
Surface Area:	15 ha (38 ac)
Mean Depth:	5.1 m (17 ft)
Max Depth:	9.9 m (33 ft)
Perimeter:	3.2 km (2 mi)
Way Point:	45° 03' 00" Lat - N
	78° 14' 00" Lon - W

Recent Fish Stocking

Year	Fish Species
1999	Rainbow trout

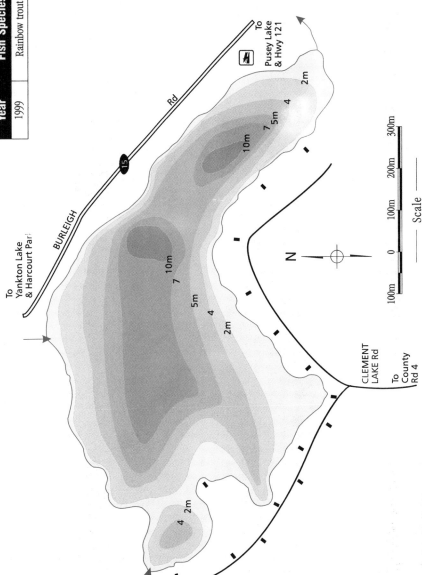

Depth Chart Not Intended for Navigational Use

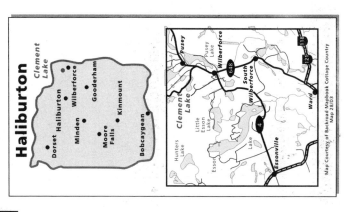

Map Courtesy of Backroad Mapbook Cottage Country Map 28/03

Contau Lake

Access

Contau Lake is located west of the village of Gooderham via the Contau Lake Road. The Contau Lake Road can be reached off County Road 507 just south of Gooderham. The road passes by the Contau Lake Dam on the northeastern shore, where a rough boat access is available near the dam site.

Facilities

Within minutes of Contau Lake, the village of Gooderham offers accommodations and other amenities.

Fishing

With an average depth of less than 2 m (6.5 ft), Contau Lake is a shallow lake. The shallow nature of the lake allows for plenty of light penetration to the lake bottom creating plenty of weed growth throughout the open water months. The heavy weed growth provides fantastic cover for all species present in the lake.

Fishing for smallmouth bass is fair to good at times from smallmouth that average around 0.5 kg (1 lb) and can be found much bigger. Smallmouth hold under the deep cover of weed beds and can often be enticed to strike by stripping a weedless fly or lure through the weeds. In the evening, smallmouth can also be drawn to strike top water popper presentations.

Walleye and muskellunge are the two other sportfish species found in Contau Lake. Fishing for walleye is fair at times, although it can be quite slow throughout parts of the season. Ice fishing for walleye is often more productive, but do not rule out casting crankbaits and other minnow imitation lures along weed lines. Muskellunge fishing is usually slow. While the large predator may not be abundant, determined musky anglers can have decent success. Walleye can be found up to 2.5 kg (5.5 lbs) in size, while musky in the 4-6 kg (9-13 lb) range are present in the lake.

Other Options

Salerno Lake is a popular cottage destination lake that lies to the southwest. It offers similar fishing opportunities as Contau Lake, with smallmouth bass, walleye and muskellunge present.

Lake Definition

Elevation:	319 m (1,063 ft)
Surface Area:	130 ha (325 ac)
Mean Depth:	1.74 m (5.8 ft)
Max Depth:	7.5 m (25 ft)
Perimeter:	13.1 km (8.2 mi)
Way Point:	44° 53' 00" Lat - N
	78° 26' 00" Lon - W

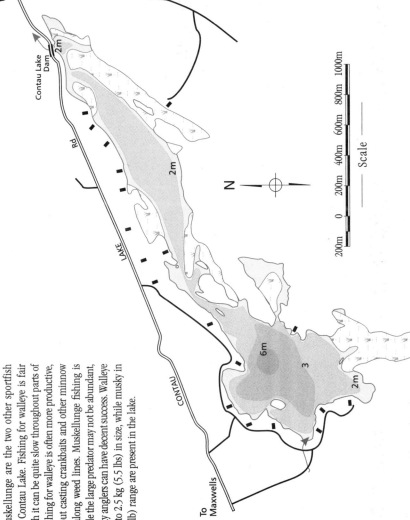

Map Courtesy of Backroad Mapbook Cottage Country Map 27/G7

Depot Lake

Access

Set within the heart of the Haliburton Forest Reserve, Depot Lake can be found by following the North Road within the Haliburton Forest. To reach the Haliburton Forest, follow the Kennisis Lake Road (County Road 7) north from Highway 118. At the gatehouse, a map to Depot Lake will be provided.

Fishing

This Haliburton Forest Reserve lake is stocked every few years with splake, which provide for good fishing at times. Depot Lake receives less pressure than many of the other lakes in the reserve; therefore, some decent sized splake can be found in this lake.

Ice fishing is one of the more popular angling methods on the lake, but spring fishing is also a productive time. During summer, splake like to retreat to the depth of the lake and fishing is rather slow. Fishing does pick up again in the fall. During the open water season, trolling with spoons east of the prominent hump in the middle of the lake can be effective. However, anglers should not rule out spinners, especially earlier and later in the season.

There are rumours that a natural population of brook trout remains in Depot Lake. It is unclear whether these reports were simply splake that were mistaken for brook trout.

Lake Definition

Surface Area: 45 ha (113 ac)
Mean Depth: 11 m (36 ft)
Max Depth: 20.4 m (70 ft)
Way Point: 45° 17' 59" Lat - N
78° 32' 05" Lon - W

Facilities

The Haliburton Forest Reserve has plenty to offer visitors, including lodge and cabin accommodations, a basic general store and rustic camping. Depot Lake itself has drive-in access camping available. For more information on the Haliburton Forest Reserve, check out www.haliburtonforest.com.

Other Options

Just to the east of Depot Lake lies **Raden Lake**. Raden Lake is stocked periodically with brook trout. Access to the lake is via a rough trail that is best traversed on foot, snowmobile or ATV.

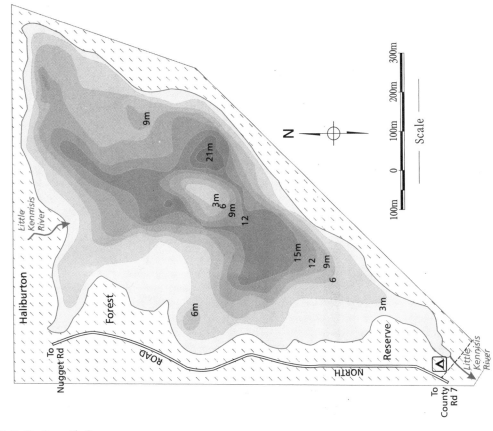

Depot Lake

N

Scale

100m   0   100m   200m   300m

Haliburton

Dorset · Hallburton · Wilberforce
Minden · Gooderham
Moore Falls · Kinmount
Bobcaygeon

Depot Lake

Sunday Lake
Raden Lake
Dutton Lake
Black Lake
Wren Lake
Duck Lake
Wolf Lake
Clean Lake
MacDonald Lake
Little Kennisis Lake
Kennisis Lake

Map Courtesy of Backroad Mapbook Cottage Country
Map 34/D5

Drag Lake

Access

This large lake lies minutes east of Haliburton and can be accessed from its southern or northwestern shore. To find the southern access, follow Highway 121 east to Long Lake Road and head north. Long Lake Road quickly passes Jones Drive, which travels west to a boat launch along the southern shore of the lake.

The northwestern access can be reached by taking Harburn Road (County Road 19) north from Haliburton to Indian Point Road. Head east on Indian Point Road and watch for boat launch signs.

Other Options

A few fishing alternatives found near Drag Lake are **Cranberry Lake** and **Boyne Lake**. Both lakes can be accessed not far off the west side of the Harburn Road (County Road 19) and offer fishing opportunities for decent sized smallmouth bass.

Fishing

Drag Lake is one of the more popular lakes in the Haliburton area and is a busy cottage destination lake during the summer months. This clear lake is extremely deep with a maximum depth of 54 m (180 ft). The crisp cool nature of the lake is prime habitat for lake trout. Fishing success for these naturally reproducing fish is definitely better in the winter months and just after ice off. Jigging small spoons along shoal areas can be effective for finding winter lakers. Due to an abundance of baitfish in Drag Lake, its resident trout can grow to good sizes and fish in the 65 cm (26 in) range are caught on occasion.

The rocky shoreline structure of Drag Lake is also fantastic smallmouth bass habitat. Smallmouth can be found in good numbers around the lake and can exceed 1.5 kg (3.5 lbs) on occasion. Due to the clear nature of the water, it is a challenge to entice smallmouth up to the top for surface lures and flies. Spincasters should try jigs and spinners, while fly casters can have great results with crayfish or leech patterns when worked around shoreline structure.

In order to protect the long term viability of the lake trout population, slot size and winter ice fishing regulations have been established. Be sure to check your regulations for details.

Facilities

Along with the main access areas, there are a few resorts and a picnic area available on Drag Lake. Alternatively, the nearby town of Haliburton offers amenities such as accommodations, restaurants and an array of retailers to service most needs.

Lake Definition

Elevation: 348 m (1,161 ft)
Surface Area: 1,003 ha (2,508 ac)
Mean Depth: 17.7 m (59.0 ft)
Max Depth: 54 m (180 ft)
Perimeter: 41.7 km (26.1 mi)
Way Point: 45° 05' 00" Lat - N
78° 24' 00" Lon - W

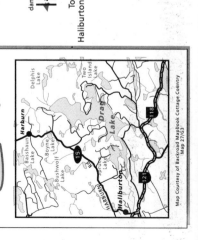

Haliburton

Dorset • Drag Lake
Haliburton • Wilberforce
Minden • Gooderham
Moore Falls • Kinmount
Bobcaygeon

Delphis Lake
Two Island Lake
Harburn
Basshaur Lake
Boyne Lake
Bushwolf Lake
Drag Lake
Haliburton

Map Courtesy of Backroad Mapbook Cottage Country Map 27/63

Duck Lake

Access

Access to Duck Lake is via a private road or trail from Redstone Lake. Owners of private property in the area have permitted access to the lake in the past and since the lake is stocked with government funded fish, there should remain public access in the future. Please do not trespass without permission from landowners.

Fishing

Duck Lake is stocked regularly with brook trout and fishing can be good, especially in the winter or spring. Through the ice, brookies can be caught by jigging small spoons along shoals in the 4-8m (13-26ft) range. In the spring, trout can be coaxed to hit fly presentations such as small bead head nymphs, Muddler Minnows and leech patterns.

It is thought that a natural population of lake trout once existed in Duck Lake. However, it is unknown if angling pressure or pollution played a role in the lake trout's demise in this lake.

Recent Fish Stocking

Year	Fish Species	Number
2001	Brook trout	1,900
2000	Brook trout	1,900
1999	Brook trout	1,900

Other Options

Dog Lake lies to the east along the same private access road; therefore, please respect landowner's wishes. Dog Lake is stocked periodically with brook trout and provides similar fishing opportunities as Duck Lake.

Facilities

No facilities exist at Duck Lake.

Lake Definition

Elevation:	371 m (1,237 ft)
Surface Area:	19 ha (48 ac)
Mean Depth:	8.1 m (27 ft)
Max Depth:	22.5 m (75 ft)
Perimeter:	3.2 km (2 mi)
Way Point:	45° 13' 00" Lat - N
	78° 31' 00" Lon - W

N

— Scale —

100m   0   100m   200m

1m
2
4m
6
8m
10
12m
16
20m
24

Trail to a private road & Redstone Lake

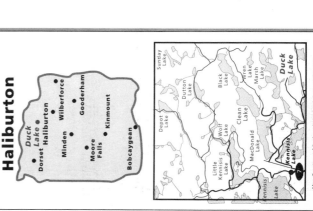

Haliburton

Dutton Lake

Access

Set in the heart of the Haliburton Forest Reserve, Dutton Lake is an interior lake that lies to the east of Little Kennisis Lake. The main route to the Haliburton Forest Reserve is to take Highway 118 to the Kennisis Lake Road (County Road 7). Follow the Kennisis Lake Road north to the Haliburton Forest Reserve gatehouse where further directions can be found.

Lake Definition

Surface Area: 61 ha (150 ac)
Mean Depth: 9.1 m (30 ft)
Max Depth: 21.3 m (70 ft)
Way Point: 45° 16' 00" Lat - N
78° 31' 00" Lon - W

Fishing

Dutton Lake is stocked every few years with splake. Fishing success for splake is best in the winter, although spring and late fall are also fine times to try for these brook trout/lake trout hybrids. Splake in Dutton Lake average around 35-40 cm (14-16 in) in size, although are caught bigger on occasion. Jigging spoons or smaller sized white jigs can work well for splake through the ice. In particular, work the shoal areas around the small islands. Trolling with spoons around the three deeper holes is the best method of fishing during the open water season.

Facilities

The Haliburton Forest Reserve is a fantastic year round recreation area that includes lodge and cabin accommodations, a basic general store and rustic camping. Drive-in access camping is available along the shore of Dutton Lake. For more information on the Haliburton Forest Reserve, check out www.haliburtonforest.com.

Other Options

If you are looking for an angling alternative to Dutton Lake, Beaver Lake and Wolf Lake lie to the west. **Beaver Lake** is a small pond like lake that lies south of Wolf Lake and is inhabited by smallmouth bass. **Wolf Lake** is stocked periodically with splake and also holds a good population of smallmouth bass. Brook trout are also rumoured to remain in the lake.

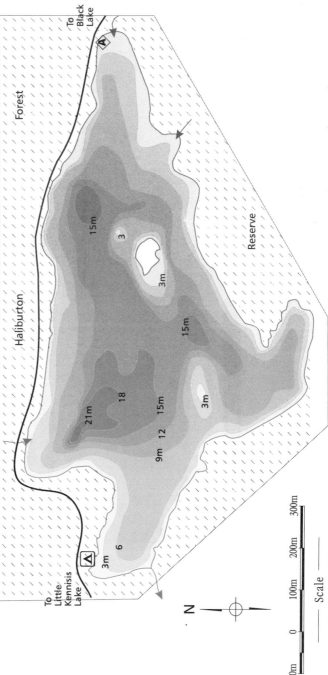

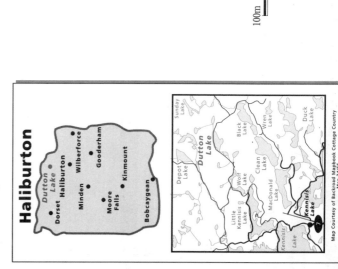

32

Eagle Lake

Access

North of Haliburton, Eagle Lake can be reached via the Eagle Lake Road (County Road 14) north off Highway 118. Eagle Lake Road leads directly to the southern shore of Eagle Lake and the boat access area at the Eagle Lake Dam.

Other Options

There are several fishing options near Eagle Lake such as **Moose Lake** to the east and **Glen Lake** to the south. Moose Lake also holds a natural population of lake trout and smallmouth bass, while the much smaller Glen Lake is home to a smallmouth bass population.

Fishing

The Redstone River flows in and out of Eagle Lake, which is controlled by a water level dam at both the entrance and exit of the lake. This constant 'flushing' of the lake brings plenty of nutrients to the lake providing ample food for baitfish and insects. In return, the resident sportfish have plenty to feed on.

Smallmouth bass are the most predominant sportfish found in the lake and provide for fair to good fishing. Smallmouth up to 1.5 kg (3.5 lbs) are often caught along shoreline areas, although the area around the small island in the middle of the lake is a favourite holding spot for bass. Brighter coloured lures and flies such as white or chartreuse seem to do well for smallmouth in this murky coloured lake.

Along with smallmouth bass, a natural population of lake trout remains in Eagle Lake. Ice fishing is still permitted on the lake and perhaps the most successful method of finding lakers. During the summer months, trolling spoons with a downrigger is really your only chance of finding these deep holding trout. Look for lake trout to hold around the deepest portions of the lake during the hotter periods. Please check your regulations before fishing Eagle Lake, as there are slot size and other special angling restrictions in place to protect fragile lake trout stocks.

Facilities

Along with several other amenities in the surrounding area, the Sir Sam's Inn is a popular all season recreation destination on Eagle Lake. South of Eagle Lake, visitors can enjoy the downhill ski hill and year round recreation trails maintained by the inn.

Lake Definition

Elevation:	343 m (1,143 ft)
Surface Area:	235 ha (588 ac)
Mean Depth:	6.8 m (22.9 ft)
Max Depth:	24 m (80 ft)
Perimeter:	10 km (6 mi)
Way Point:	45° 08' 00" Lat - N
	78° 31' 00" Lon - W

Recent Fish Stocking

Year	Fish Species
1996	Lake trout

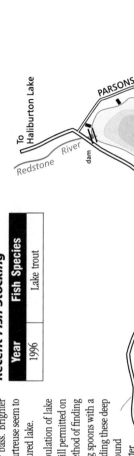

Depth Chart Not Intended for Navigational Use

Map Courtesy of Backroad Mapbook Cottage Country Map 27/E1

Eels Lake

Access

The main access point to Eels Lake is located north of the village of Apsley. Just south of Silent Lake Provincial Park, look for the Eels Lake Public Landing Road off the west side of Highway 28.

Other Options

If the action on Eels Lake is a little too slow, you can always head over to the Monmouth Lakes. **Monmouth Lake** and **Lower Monmouth Lake** lie just beyond the northwestern end of Eels Lake. Monmouth Lake is stocked annually with lake trout, while both lakes provide for decent fishing for smallmouth bass.

Fishing

Eels Lake is one of the larger lakes in the region and is a popular Cottage Country destination. The lake has some very interesting shoreline and underwater structure. The many islands and bays found around the lake make for ideal bass habitat, as smallmouth and largemouth bass frequent these areas. Smallmouth are much more common than largemouth and provide for good fishing at times. Bass average about 1 kg (2 lbs) in size, although they can be found exceeding 1.5 kg (3.5 lbs).

A natural population of lake trout also exists in Eels Lake. These fish are the more popular sportfish in the lake and can exceed 65 cm (26 in) in size on occasion. The most productive time of year to try for lake trout is in the winter through the ice or in the spring, just after ice off. The size and odd shape of the lake can make it difficult to locate the lake trout. In the spring, lakers can be almost anywhere around the lake; however, they tend to concentrate close to the deeper portions of the lake.

In order to help preserve the natural lake trout population of Eels Lake, slot size and winter ice fishing restrictions are in place. Please check the provincial fishing regulations for details.

Facilities

Visitors to Eels Lake will find that there are a number of accommodations available on the lake such as resorts, lodges and rental cottages. Supplies can be picked up in the village of Apsley.

Lake Definition

Elevation:	352 m (1,155 ft)
Surface Area:	1,021 ha (2,337 ac)
Mean Depth:	6.7 m (22 ft)
Max Depth:	42.7 m (98 ft)
Perimeter:	62 km (39 mi)
Way Point:	44° 54' 00" Lat - N
	78° 08' 00" Lon - W

Haliburton

Dorset • Haliburton
• Minden • Wilberforce
Moore • Gooderham
Falls • Kinmount
• Bobcaygeon

Eels Lake

Map Courtesy of Backroad Mapbook Cottage Country
Map 28/37

Scale

400m 0 400m 800m 1200m 1600m

N

To Paudash Lake
To Apsley
28

To Dyno Rd/ Hwy 648
Farrel Cr.
Eels Cr.
ROAD
LAKE
EELS
WEST
Eels Lake Dam
Eels Cr.
To Hwy 28
EELS LAKE Rd
Higgins Cr.
To West Eels Lake Rd
To Hwy 28
Devils Isl.
Fox Isls
Picnic Isl
Cow Isl
Loon Isl

Elephant Lake

Access

Elephant Lake is a large, scenic lake that lies within minutes of the southern tip of Algonquin Provincial Park. The lake can be found by following Highway 121 to Highway 648. Travel north along the 648 to the Elephant Lake Road (County Road 10) and continue north. Shortly along the Elephant Lake Road, there is an access point available along the western shore of the lake.

Other Options

Benoir Lake to the north, is linked to Elephant Lake via the York River and is accessible by boat. Since Benoir Lake is so closely tied to the larger Elephant Lake, anglers can expect similar fishing opportunities. Smallmouth bass, largemouth bass, muskellunge and walleye are all present in Benoir Lake.

Fishing

Elephant Lake was originally known as Mud Lake and later as Shawahkong Lake. In the late 1800's, the lake began to be called Elephant Lake due to its odd Elephant-like shape. There are numerous cottages and camps on Elephant Lake, but the fishing remains consistent. Success is best for both smallmouth and largemouth bass. Bass average 0.5-1 kg (1-2 lbs) in size and can be found much larger in the lake. The many weed beds found around the lake are a haven for aggressive bass.

Walleye are the most sought after species in Elephant Lake and fishing is generally fair for walleye that average 1 kg (2 lbs). Throughout the season, trolling along weed lines can be effective. The massive shoal areas located in the middle of the lake and off the eastern most island are also fantastic areas for attracting baitfish and eventually predators like walleye.

A population of muskellunge can also be found in Elephant Lake and fishing is known to be decent at times. The best chance to hook into one of these mighty fish is in the fall when they are most apt to strike on standard presentations.

Facilities

A number of resorts and cottages line the shore of Elephant Lake helping overnight visitors enjoy the natural beauty of the area. The lake is also a great place to drop the boat in for the day. The Kingscote Lake access to Algonquin Provincial Park is minutes north of Elephant Lake. Visit www.OntarioParks.com for more information.

Lake Definition

Elevation:	347 m (1,157 ft)
Surface Area:	87 ha (2,186 ac)
Mean Depth:	1.8 m (6 ft)
Max Depth:	8 m (26 ft)
Perimeter:	34 km (21 mi)
Way Point:	45° 08' 00" Lat - N
	78° 08' 00" Lon - W

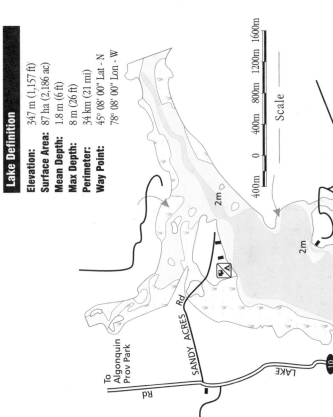

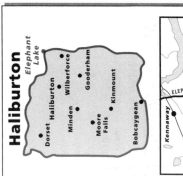

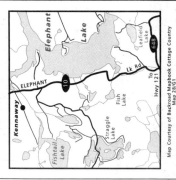

Elephant Lake

Esson (Otter) Lake

Access

East of Haliburton, Esson or Otter Lake can be reached by following Highway 121 to County Road 4. County Road 4 continues east eventually passing by the southern end of the lake and a boat launch area.

Lake Definition

Elevation:	427 m (1,423 ft)
Surface Area:	24 ha (60 ac)
Mean Depth:	10.7 m (35.9 ft)
Max Depth:	30 m (100 ft)
Perimeter:	17 km (11 mi)
Way Point:	45° 01' 00" Lat - N
	78° 16' 00" Lon - W

Fishing

Smallmouth bass provide the bulk of the action on Esson Lake and success for bass can be good at times for fish up to 1.5 kg (3.5 lbs). The north and south ends of Esson Lake are regarded as the best areas for finding bass, as there is plenty of rock and weed structure providing good cover. Another good area for smallmouth can be around the shallow 'neck' of the lake near its northern end. In this area, the lake is separated into two areas by a shallower area. Underwater rock and weed structure is prevalent in this region making for prime bass habitat.

A natural population of lake trout also exists in Esson Lake. However, the long-term viability of the species is in question, as shoreline development, pollution and over fishing are having negative effects on this fragile species. Over the past few years, a stocking program has been established to supplement existing stocks and to help maintain the fishery. Special slot size and ice fishing regulations have also been established. Please practice catch and release to aid the ailing natural lake trout population.

Other Options

Little Esson Lake is located to the northeast via a 2wd road. The smaller lake provides fishing opportunities for smallmouth bass and stocked rainbow trout.

Facilities

Basic amenities are available in the nearby village of Wilberforce.

Recent Fish Stocking

Year	Fish Species	Number
2002	Lake trout	2,325
2001	Lake trout	2,300
2000	Lake trout	2,300

Farquhar Lake

Access

North of the village of Wilberforce, Farquhar Lake can be reached via two access roads that branch north off Highway 648. A private access area is available at the southern end of the lake and can be used by visitors for a fee.

Other Options

A small lake named **Pine Lake** lies just to the west of Farquhar Lake and can be accessed by a rough road/trail from the north. Pine Lake was once stocked with rainbow trout, but only a natural population of lake trout remains in the lake. While the size and success may not be fantastic, this little lake is worth the visit simply for its seclusion and beauty. Watch for special fishing regulations on this lake.

Fishing

When settlement first began in the Haliburton area, many lakes were eventually named after officials of the historic Canada Land and Emigration Company. Farquhar Lake is no different as it was named after an officer from the British company that was a major player in helping develop the Haliburton area in the mid 1800's.

Farquhar Lake looks like a prime lake trout lake and it produced quite well for lake trout decades ago. However, over the years steady fishing pressure and development of the lake has dwindled stocks. A population of natural lake trout remains in the lake, but fishing success is generally slow.

Anglers looking for some decent action should focus their efforts on its resident smallmouth bass population. Fishing for smallmouth is regarded as fair for bass that average around 1 kg (2 lbs) in size. Shoreline rock structure is a good area to look for smallmouth, especially off the small island found on the lake. Subsurface flies and lures are recommended due to the clear nature of the lake.

Additionally, anglers should be aware that a small dam found on its southern end regulates the lake level. Depending on water needs in the Trent Canal system, water levels can fluctuate up to 2.5 m (8 ft). This definitely affects shoreline structure and the quality of fishing.

Facilities

Various accommodations are available in the Wilberforce area such as rental cottages and privately run campgrounds.

Lake Definition

Mean Depth: 24 m (80 ft)
Max Depth: 49 m (163 ft)
Way Point: 45° 05' 00" Lat - N
78° 12' 00" Lon - W

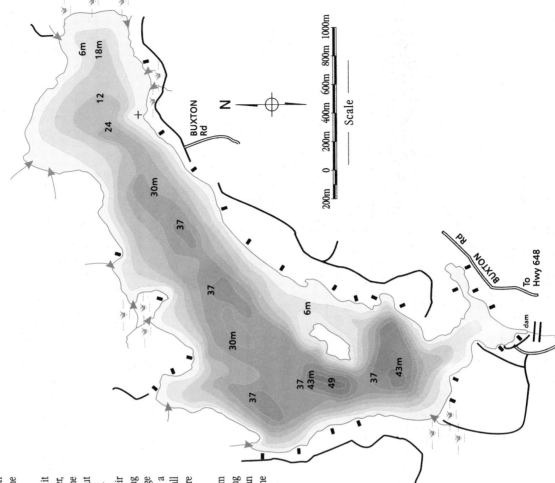

Depth Chart Not Intended for Navigational Use

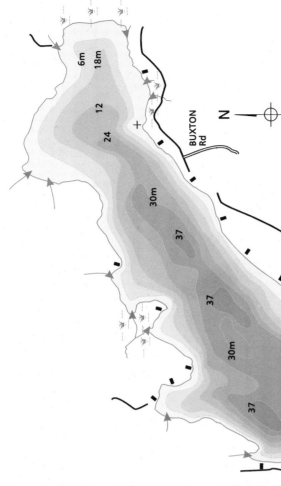

Map Courtesy of Backroad Mapbook Cottage Country Map 28/E2

Fishog Lake

Access

Fishog Lake is located northeast of the popular Head Lake and northwest of the village of Norland. There is currently no designated public access to the lake, as the roads leading near the southern tip of the lake are private. A few resorts in the area do offer access to the lake. Your best bet to find info on these resorts is to inquire locally in the village of Norland. Please do not trespass on private property.

Fishing

Splake have been regularly stocked in Fishog Lake up until 1999 and it is unclear whether the lake will be stocked regularly again in the future. Splake have provided decent fishing opportunities over the years but this sterile crossbreed is unable to reproduce and cannot survive without consistent stocking. Anglers looking for splake are advised to work the deeper hole in the western arm of the lake.

Fishog Lake does hold a good population of bass. Fishing for smallmouth and largemouth bass can be good throughout the season for bass that average about 1 kg (2 lbs) in size. The narrows between the west and east sections of the lake are a good place to look for ambush ready bass.

It is also reported that a resident population of muskellunge is also resident in the lake, although angling success is undetermined.

Facilities

A few resorts in the area offer access and amenities on Fishog Lake, as well as guided access to a number of other lakes in the area. The nearby village of Norland also has plenty to offer visitors, including accommodations, restaurants and other retail outlets.

Other Options

Lower Digby Lake and **Cranberry Lake** are two remote access lakes that lie to the north of Fishog Lake. The lakes are part of a small system of lakes that offer angling opportunities for both smallmouth bass and largemouth bass. The difficult access should ensure some fabulous fishing for bass that rarely see a lure.

Lake Definition

Elevation:	271 m (890 ft)
Surface Area:	87 ha (217 ac)
Mean Depth:	6 m (19.5 ft)
Max Depth:	13 m (43 ft)
Perimeter:	9 km (6 mi)
Way Point:	45° 05' 00" Lat - N
	78° 12' 00" Lon - W

Recent Fish Stocking

Year	Fish Species
1999	Splake
1997	Splake
1995	Splake

Haliburton

Dorset Haliburton Minden Wilberforce Gooderham Moore Falls Kinmount Bobcaygeon Fishog Lake

West Moore's Lake Oak Lake Beechnut Lake Norland 35 45 HILTON'S Pt Rd N Head Lake Fishog Lake

Map Courtesy of Backroad Mapbook Cottage Country Map 19/03

N

Scale

100m 0 100m 200m 300m 400m 500m

Digby Cr.

Head River

15   11m   7   4m

Fishtail Lake

Access

Fishtail Lake is located just outside of the private Harcourt Park area. To find the access to the lake, follow the Elephant Lake Road (County Road 10) north from Highway 648. After crossing Allen Creek, look for Fishtale Road branching west. This road leads past the small community of Kennaway to the north shore of the lake.

Alternatively, look for the Harcourt Park access road off the west side of the Elephant Lake Road. Take the Harcourt Park access road to the first fork in the road and proceed west along the rougher looking road (do not stay on the main road south into Harcourt Park). The rough road eventually leads to the eastern shore of Fishtail Lake and to a rustic access area.

Fishing

Originally this lake was named Trout Lake in 1855 and later in the century, the name was changed to Fishtail Lake, most probably due to the sheer number of 'Trout Lake' names that had popped up throughout the decades.

Fishtail Lake was once well known for its lake trout; however, the species has been under constant pressure and the population levels have declined. Fishing success for lake trout is now regarded as fair at times, with trolling right across the middle of the lake being the most effective method.

Smallmouth bass provide the best action on the lake as bass frequent much of the rocky shore structure around the lake. Both the northeastern and southwestern ends of the lake are the main holding areas for smallmouth. In particular, the rocky shoals along the southeastern shore are a prime habitat area.

Be sure to check the provincial regulations before heading out, as Fishtail Lake is part of the winter/spring fish sanctuary in order to help the lake trout stocks. Catch and release can go a long way in ensuring a future for these fragile sportfish.

Facilities

While there are no facilities available on Fishtail Lake, there are plenty of various amenities available on nearby Elephant Lake and in the Wilberforce area.

Lake Definition

Elevation:	393 m (1,290 ft)
Surface Area:	247 ha (610 ac)
Mean Depth:	18 m (59.2 ft)
Max Depth:	40 m (132 ft)
Perimeter:	12 km (8 mi)
Way Point:	45° 09' 00" Lat - N
	78° 12' 00" Lon - W

Other Options

A good alternative to Fishtail Lake is nearby **Kenneway Lake**. Kenneway Lake lies to the southeast of Fishtail Lake, within the private Harcourt Park area. Permission must be obtained to access the lake, which has been stocked in the past with rainbow trout.

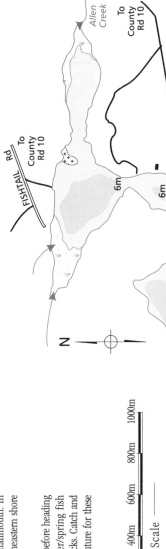

N

Allen Creek

To County Rd 10

FISHTAIL Rd

To County Rd 10

6m

6m

12

18m

24

30m

37

24

24m

24m

37

18

36

30m

24

18m

12

6m

Allen Creek

Scale

200m 0 200m 400m 600m 800m 1000m

Depth Chart Not Intended for Navigational Use

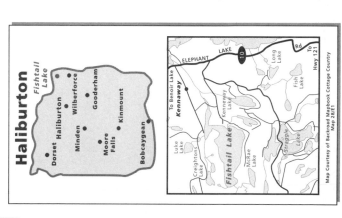

Haliburton

Fishtail Lake

Dorset Haliburton
Minden Wilberforce
Gooderham
Moore Falls Kinmount
Bobcaygean

ELEPHANT LAKE

To Benoir Lake Kennaway
Luke Lake
Creightons Lake
McRae Lake
Straggle Lake
Fishtail Lake
Long Lake
Fish Lake
Rd To Hwy 121

Map Courtesy of Backroad Mapbook Cottage Country Map 28:E1

Fletcher Lake

Access

Fletcher Lake is located north of the much larger Kawagama Lake. To find Fletcher Lake, follow Highway 35 north of Dorset to County Road 12. County Road 12 travels north eventually past the southern shore of the lake. A public access available on the Buck Bay near the western end of the lake.

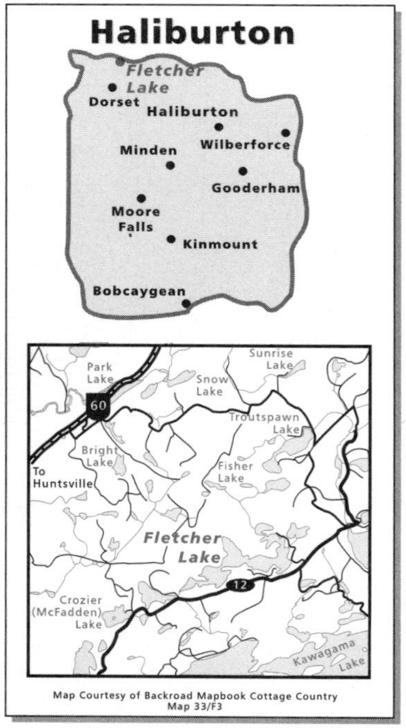

Fishing

It is rumoured that a population of brook trout once inhabited Fletcher Lake, although it is widely thought that the species is now extinct from the lake. However, anglers visiting Fletcher Lake can expect to find lake trout, which are stocked periodically. Fishing for average sized lakers is slow to fair.

In the winter, ice fishing is a popular pastime on this lake and success is usually at its best during this time. Jig off shoal areas and over any anomalies in the lake bottom such as over one of the 9 m (30 ft) humps found in the eastern end of the lake or in Buck Bay. While lake trout can be found in other areas of the lake, these two deeper ends of the lake seem to be the primary holding areas.

After ice off, anglers will experience a short window of success before resident trout head to the depths of the lake. Late in the year, as the water temperature begins to drop, lake trout will move back to the upper portions of the lake in search of food. Success is often not as good as in the spring, although much better than in the summer.

Other Options

En route to Fletcher Lake, County Road 12 passes by the southern shore of a number of lakes including **Crozier Lake** and **Lower Fletcher Lake**. Crozier Lake is inhabited by lake trout and once also supported a brook trout population, although it is unclear whether the species remains in the lake. Lower Fletcher Lake is stocked periodically with lake trout, which provide for decent angling opportunities throughout the year. Before heading out, be sure to check for any specific regulations imposed on these lakes.

Facilities

The public access point is suitable for smaller sized trailers and offers some parking. During busy periods, many visitors park along the side of the road. A picnic area is also found near the dam on the west end of the lake. Accommodations and other amenities can be found in the nearby village of Dorset.

Lake Definition

Mean Depth: 11 m (35 ft)
Max Depth: 21 m (70 ft)
Way Point: 45° 21' 00" Lat - N
78° 47' 00" Lon - W

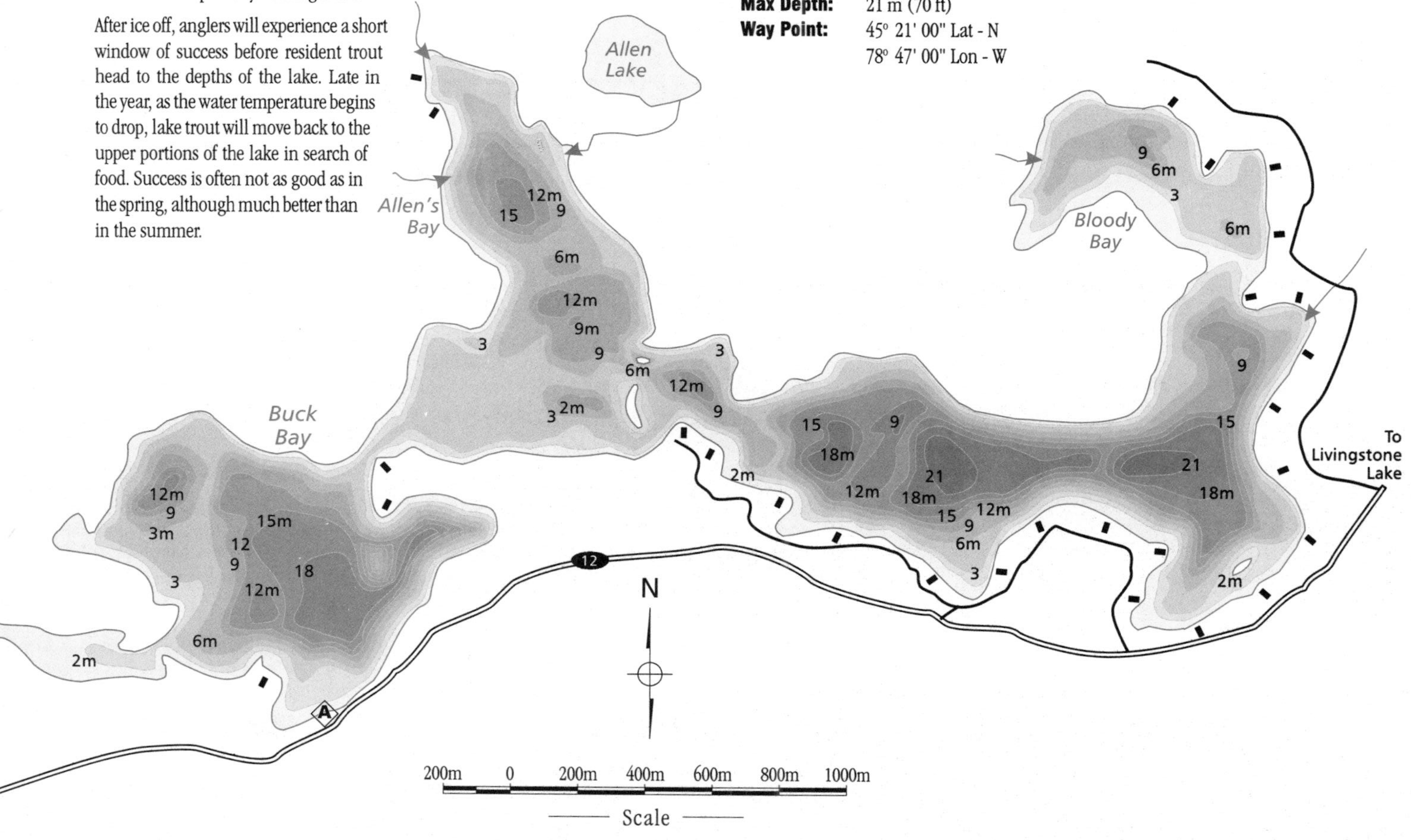

Haliburton

Fletcher Lake
Dorset Haliburton
Minden • Wilberforce
• Gooderham
Moore • Kinmount
Falls
Bobcaygeon

Sunrise Lake
Snow Lake
Troutspawn Lake
Park Lake
To Huntsville
Bright Lake
Fisher Lake
Fletcher Lake
Crozier (McFadden) Lake

Map Courtesy of Backroad Mapbook Cottage Country
Map 33/f3

Map labels

Bloody Bay
6m 6m
9 6m 3
9 21 18m 2m
15
9 12m
15 6m
21 18m 9 3
12m
9
18m
15
2m 3 9
Allen Lake
3 12m
6m
6m 9
15 12m 9
6m 9m
3 2m
Allen's Bay
3
Buck Bay
15m
12 18
9 12m
6m
12m
9 3
3m 2m
2m
Grassy Bay
2m
2m
dam
To Hwy 35
To Livingstone Lake

N

Scale
200m 0 200m 400m 600m 800m 1000m

Fourcorner Lake

Access

Fourcorner Lake is a very beautiful lake that lies partially within Algonquin Provincial Park. Access to the lake is limited to a rough 4wd road in the spring and summer or snowmobile in the winter. One of the most direct routes to the lake is to take the Harcourt Park Road (County Road 15) north off Highway 648. Within 1 km (0.6 mi) of Harcourt Park, look for a rough 4wd road leading north. This rough road is a challenge to navigate due to the extensive logging in the area. If you pick the right route, you should make it to within a few hundred metres of the southern shore of the lake. From here, it is a short bushwhack to the lake. Ardent anglers have been known to haul in a canoe to better fish this lake.

In winter, a snowmobile trail leads past the lake.

Other Options

Kingscote Lake is the southernmost access point to Algonquin Provincial Park. The popular lake offers some fantastic backcountry camping opportunities as well as fishing for lake trout and the odd brook trout. While Fourcorner Lake is not restricted by Algonquin Park's special regulations, the park regulates Kingscote Lake.

Lake Definition

Elevation:	438 m (1,460 ft)
Surface Area:	9 ha (238 ac)
Mean Depth:	7.5 m (25 ft)
Max Depth:	26.1 m (85.6 ft)
Perimeter:	7 km (4 mi)
Way Point:	45° 10' 00" Lat - N
	78° 10' 00" Lon - W

Fishing

Lake trout are stocked regularly in Fourcorner Lake and provide for good fishing through the ice in winter and in the spring just after ice off. Lake trout are usually oxygen starved during the winter; therefore, angling success is better closer to the surface of the lake. Try jigging a small spoon or jig closer to shore within the upper 6 m (20 ft) of the lake. Lakers average about 40 cm (16 in) in size although they can be found larger.

A natural population of brook trout is still rumoured to exist in the lake. These elusive fish can also be caught through the ice as well as in the spring using flies or small lures.

Facilities

The northern shore of Fourcorner Lake lies within a very remote section of Algonquin Provincial Park. Since the remaining portion of the lake is found on Crown Land, rustic backcountry camping is possible along the southern shore of the lake. Please be sure to carry out any garbage you may bring in or find while at the lake.

Recent Fish Stocking

Year	Fish Species	Number
2002	Lake Trout	1,200
2001	Lake Trout	1,000
2000	Lake Trout	1,000

Depth Chart Not Intended for Navigational Use

Map Courtesy of Backroad Mapbook Cottage Country Map 28/C1

Copyright © Mussio Ventures Ltd.

41

Glamor (Big Bear) Lake

Access

Southeast of the town of Haliburton, Glamor Lake can be reached by taking Highway 121 east from Haliburton to Buckhorn Road (County Road 3). Follow Buckhorn Road south to the Glamor Lake Road and head east. After approximately 2 km along the Glamor Lake Road, look for a road to the north. This road leads to an access point at the Glamor Lake Dam on the southeastern end of the lake.

Fishing

Glamor Lake is a very clear lake quite suitable for trout species but anglers often find better success searching for the resident smallmouth bass. Bass can be found up to 1.5 kg (3.5 lbs) in size, although they average about 0.5 kg (1 lb). Smallmouth are known to hang around the abundant shore structure around the lake, especially around the two main islands. The 6 m (20 ft) shoal just south of Big Island is also a decent holding area for bass.

A natural population of lake trout has provided good fishing on Glamor Lake for decades. Unfortunately, cottage development and over harvesting has resulted in a dramatic decline in lake trout stocks over the past several years. It is unclear if the natural lake trout population will be a part of the future of this lake. As a result, rainbow trout were stocked in the lake in late 2002 in order to provide an alternative sportfishing opportunity. Please practice catch and release and check the regulations before fishing this lake, as there are a number of special restrictions in place.

Other Options

Little Glamor Lake lies due north of Glamor Lake and also hosts a natural lake trout population as well as smallmouth bass. Fishing is better for smallmouth bass in the smaller lake.

Facilities

Accommodations and other facilities are available in the village of Gooderham to the south or the town of Haliburton to the northwest.

Lake Definition

Elevation: 365 m (1,216 ft)
Surface Area: 19 ha (48 ac)
Mean Depth: 8.6 m (28.8 ft)
Max Depth: 21 m (70 ft)
Perimeter: 11 km (7 mi)
Way Point: 45° 50' 00" Lat - N 78° 23' 00" Lon - W

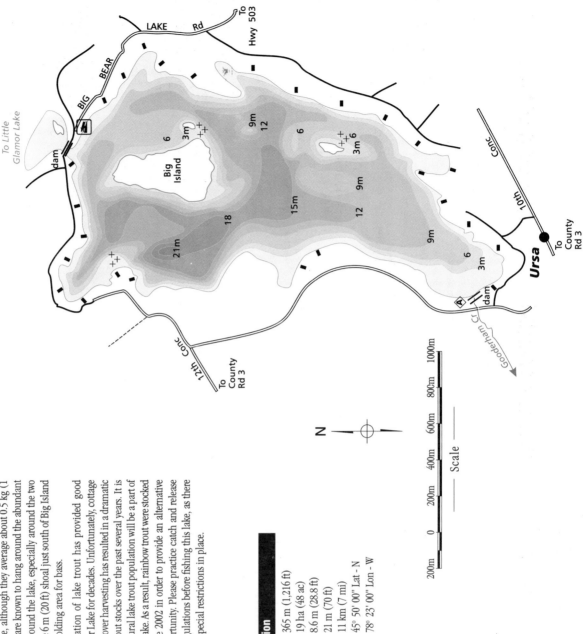

Gooderham (Pine) Lake

Access

In the village of Gooderham, Gooderham Lake can be accessed via Buckhorn Road (County Road 3) southeast of Haliburton. A boat launch area is available along the western shore of the lake off Buckhorn Road.

Lake Definition

Elevation: 299 m (997 ft)
Surface Area: 7 ha (18 ac)
Mean Depth: 6 m (20 ft)
Max Depth: 18 m (59 ft)
Perimeter: 8 km (5 mi)
Way Point: 44° 54' 00" Lat - N
78° 23' 00" Lon - W

Fishing

Although lake trout were once present and splake were once stocked in Gooderham Lake, the best bet for fishing is for the resident smallmouth bass. Smallmouth average about 1 kg (2 lbs) in size and can be found around the shore structure in the lake. Try working a tube jig or streamer off rocky shorelines or along any one of the island areas for ambush ready smallmouth.

A fair to good population of walleye can also be found in Gooderham Lake. Fishing usually picks up during the winter and can be consistent during the fall months for this prized sportfish. Through the ice, try jigging a small scented jig. During the open water season, a variety of tactics can be productive, including trolling a worm harness along shore structure. However, casting a jig is always fun, as it often grabs the attention of both bass and walleye.

Other Options

Just north of Gooderham Lake lies the small lake named **Little Bob Lake**. Little Bob Lake is a scenic Haliburton Lake that is stocked every few years with brook trout and makes a fine fishing destination.

Facilities

The village of Gooderham offers a few amenities for area visitors to enjoy. For full services, the town of Haliburton is found only minutes away to the northwest.

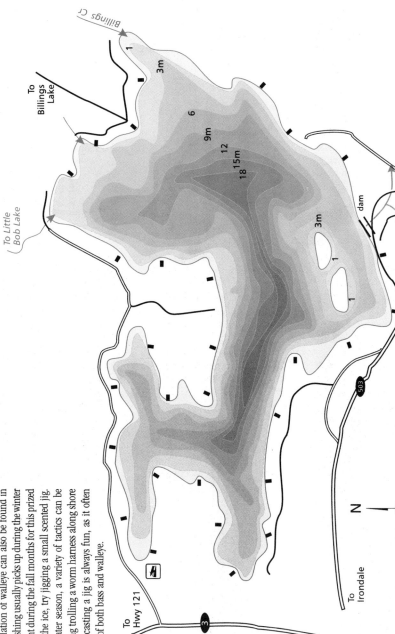

Scale
100m 0 100m 200m 300m 400m 500m

Depth Chart Not Intended for Navigational Use

Haliburton

Dorset
Wilberforce
Haliburton
Minden   Gooderham
Moore   Kinmount
Falls
Bobcaygeon

Map Courtesy of Backroad Mapbook Cottage Country
Map 28/A7

Gull Lake (North)

Access

Set between the town of Minden and the settlement of Moore Falls, Gull Lake lies off the west side of Highway 35. While it is possible to launch a canoe from the side of the road, it is not recommended. Boat launching is limited to mainly in Miners Bay and from a few of the resorts found around the lake.

Fishing

Reference to Gull Lake dates back as far as 1826 when it was named Kinashingiquash Lake. It is not certain when the name was changed, although the name selection certainly was in reference to the Gull River, which flows in and out of Gull Lake. This big lake is a popular cottage country destination and has many camps and cottages scattered along its shoreline.

Lake trout are perhaps the most sought after sportfish on Gull Lake and a natural population of lake trout remains in the lake. Fishing is best during the winter ice fishing season and hold until just after ice off. Fishing can be decent for a few weeks before lakers head for deeper waters. Trolling with downriggers is the only effective summertime trout angling method.

Gull Lake also holds both smallmouth and largemouth bass. Fishing for bass can be good at times for bass that average 1 kg (2 lbs) in size, although they can be found much larger. There is plenty of fine bass structure found around the big lake and anglers should work the weedy bays, the rocky drop-offs or even the man-made structure such as boat docks. Spincasters should try jigs and spinners, while fly casters can have great results with crayfish or leech patterns when worked around shoreline structure.

In order to protect the natural lake trout population of Gull Lake, slot size restrictions and special ice fishing regulations have been established. Check the provincial fishing regulations summary for details and please practice catch and release for these fragile trout.

Lake Definition

Elevation:	243 m (810 ft)
Surface Area:	80 ha (198 ac)
Mean Depth:	14.7 m (49 ft)
Max Depth:	44.1 m (147 ft)
Perimeter:	30 km (19 mi)
Way Point:	44° 51' 00" Lat - N
	78° 47' 00" Lon - W

Scale

400m 0 400m 800m 1200m 1600m

N

Gull Lake
-North End

Gull Lake (South)

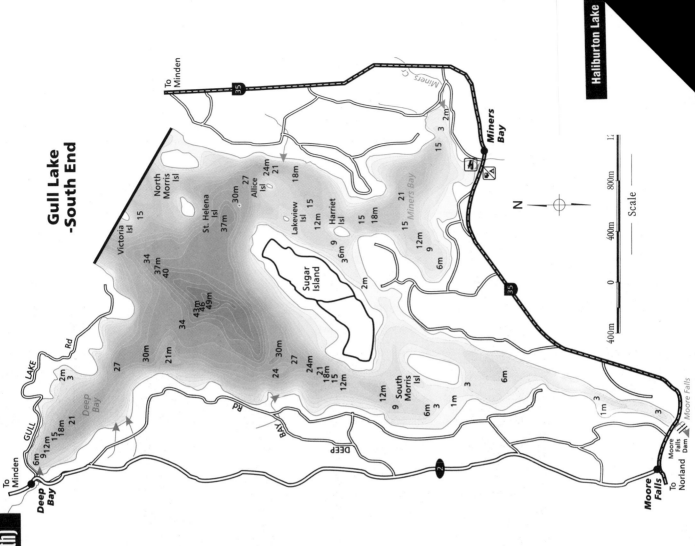

Gull Lake - South End

Facilities

There are a few resorts and lodges available on and around Gull Lake as well as several rental cottages available (inquire locally). Supplies can be found in the town of Minden minutes away to the north.

Other Options

North Pigeon and **Little Bob Lakes** are located near the northwestern shore of Gull Lake and are accessible via 2wd roads. The smaller lakes are stocked every few years with lake trout and are home to resident smallmouth and largemouth bass populations. A privately run campground lies on Little Bob Lake

Haliburton

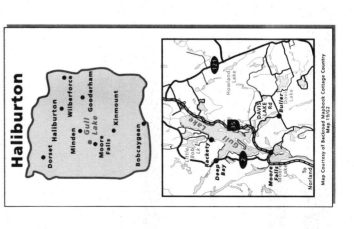

Map Courtesy of Backroad Mapbook Cottage Country Map 19/G2

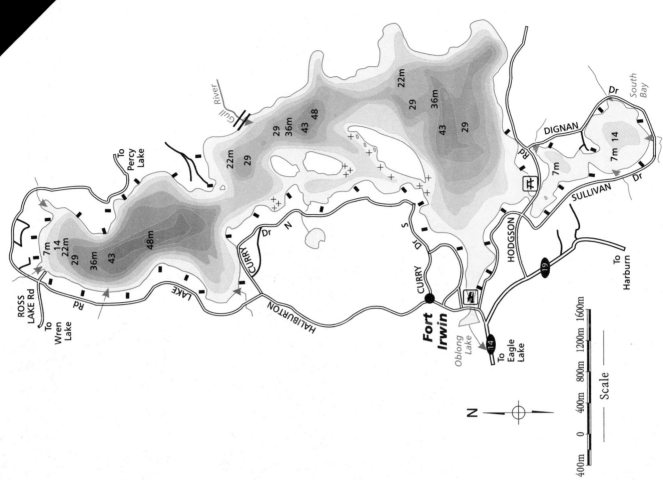

Haliburton Lake

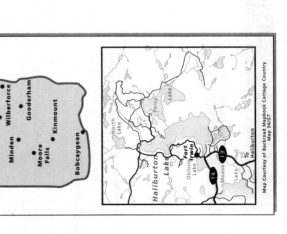

Access

Haliburton Lake is located northeast of the town of Haliburton and can be reached by following the Harburn Road (County Road 19) north from the town of Haliburton. Public access is available at the southwestern end of the lake, at the settlement of Fort Irwin. Fort Irwin lies near the junction of County 19 and County Road 14.

Other Options

Oblong Lake can be reached from Haliburton Lake by water from its southwestern end. Oblong Lake offers much of the same fishing opportunities as Haliburton Lake and is part of the winter/spring fishing sanctuary period to help natural lake trout stocks.

Fishing

This large cottage lake is a popular summer destination with several cottages and a few resorts along its shoreline. The deep clear nature (measuring over 55 m (180 ft) in one area of the lake) makes ideal habitat for lake trout. Although they are preferred sportfish for area anglers, fishing for these self-sustaining trout is fair at best throughout the year.

Success for smallmouth bass is much better than for lake trout for bass that average 0.5-1 kg (1-2 lbs). The abundance of rock shoals and drop-offs around the lake make for prime smallmouth habitat. One of the most effective flies and lures on this lake is a crayfish imitation. Working a crayfish fly or grub close to bottom structure in a jerky motion, closely imitates the escape of a crayfish. The larger smallmouth bass can often be fooled into taking this type of presentation.

Be sure to check for any special regulations on this lake.

Facilities

In addition to a boat launch and picnic site found at the south end, there are a few resorts around the lake for overnight visitors to enjoy. The town of Haliburton also offers overnight accommodations as well as any needed supplies.

Lake Definition

Elevation:	355 m (1,182 ft)
Surface Area:	100 ha (247 ac)
Mean Depth:	17.1 m (57.2 ft)
Max Depth:	54 m (180 ft)
Perimeter:	6 km (4 mi)
Way Point:	45° 12' 00" Lat - N
	78° 24' 00" Lon - W

HIGHLAND Rd

To Carnarvon

35

7m
15
22m
29
44 51m
37m
29
15 22m
7m
59
51m
44
29 37m
66m 73 80m
22m
15
7m

Halls Lake Dam

Buttermilk Falls

LAKE Rd

13

HALLS

Halls Lake
To Dorset

35

N

Scale

200m 0 200m 400m 600m 800m 1000m

Halls Lake

Access

North of the village of Carnarvon, Halls Lake is easily accessible off Highway 35. A boat launch is available not far off the highway, while another access point is available off Highland Road along the east side of the lake.

Other Options

Anglers looking for a change from the popular lakefront of Halls Lake can always venture over to Saskatchewan Lake. **Saskatchewan Lake** is a small lake that lies within the Leslie M. Frost Centre and is located northwest of Halls Lake off Highway 35. This small lake is inhabited with both smallmouth and largemouth bass providing for some consistent actions at times.

Fishing

This round shaped lake is quite deep and is home to several scenic cottages. The easy access and popularity of the lake results in high fishing pressure throughout the year; however, success for smallmouth bass remains fair. Bass average 0.5-1 kg (1-2 lbs) and can be found up to 1.5 kg (3.5 lbs) in size. Working the rocky shore structure of the lake with a tube jig or streamer type fly can provide results.

Halls Lake is also home to a population of lake trout. Fishing Dorset for lake trout is generally slow throughout the year and is best through the ice or in the spring just after ice off. Slot size and ice fishing restrictions are in place on the lake. Please consult the fishing regulations for exact details.

Facilities

In addition to the two boat launches, there is a picnic area found near the boat launch on the southwest side of the lake. Resorts, accommodations and supplies can be found at the nearby villages of Carnarvon or Dorset. Carnarvon lies to the south of Halls Lake and the village of Dorset is located north of the lake. Also found to the north is the Leslie M. Frost Centre. This is the main Ontario Ministry of Natural Resources training centre that also doubles as a fantastic outdoor recreation area. Rustic backcountry campsites, trails and canoe routes help make this centre the popular retreat that it is.

Lake Definition

Elevation: 321 m (1,069 ft)
Surface Area: 53 ha (133 ac)
Mean Depth: 43.8 m (143.7 ft)
Max Depth: 80.4 m (264 ft)
Way Point: 45° 06' 00" Lat - N
78° 45' 00" Lon - W

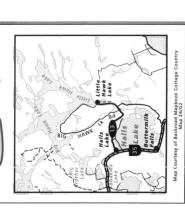

Haliburton

Dorset
Halls Haliburton
Lake Minden
Wilberforce
Gooderham
Moore Falls
Kinmount
Bobcaygeon

Little Hawk Lake

BIG HAWK Lk Rd

Halls Lake

Halls Lake

Buttermilk Falls

35

Map Courtesy of Backroad Mapbook Cottage Country
Map 28/G2

Havelock Lake

Access

Havelock Lake lies in the northern boundary of the Haliburton Forest Reserve; therefore, a road access permit is required to travel to the lake. The main entrance to the Haliburton Forest Reserve can be reached near the end of the Kennisis Lake Road (County Road 7). Follow the road signs to the permit office. They will provide road and/or trail directions into Havelock Lake.

Fishing

This blueish, green coloured lake looks like the perfect trout lake but anglers will need to study the hydrographic makeup of the lake to find these elusive fish. There are essentially three prime holding areas for lake trout in Havelock Lake, the northern end, the southwestern arm and the deep western arm.

The northern portion of the lake is quite interesting because there are two deep basins separated by a 12 m (40 ft) hump. During the open water season, trolling from the deep areas back and forth across this hump can produce results. In the southwestern arm, lakers will hold in the deep hole and will rise to the 12 m (40 ft) range on occasion to feed. The western arm of Havelock Lake is the deepest portion of the lake and regularly holds lake trout during the warmer periods of the season.

If you plan on heading out on Havelock Lake in the winter, it is best to focus your efforts off shoal areas. Many anglers prefer to ice fish off the 1.5 m (5 ft) shoal found in the middle of Havelock Lake. Jigging a small jig or spoon in deeper water beside the shoal can be very effective.

Before heading out, check the regulations. There are slot size and special ice fishing restrictions in place to maintain the lake trout population.

Lake Definition

Elevation: 374 m (1,245 ft)
Surface Area: 16 ha (40 ac)
Mean Depth: 9 m (30 ft)
Max Depth: 30 m (100 ft)
Perimeter: 16 km (10 mi)
Way Point: 45° 17' 00" Lat - N
78° 38' 00" Lon - W

Facilities

The Haliburton Forest Reserve is a privately run outdoor recreation paradise. The area offers everything from cabin rentals to a full service lodge. Rustic campsites are available throughout the reserve and can be used for a fee. On Havelock Lake, there is a scenic picnic area available along the eastern shore of the lake.

Other Options

A much smaller angling alternative is **Snap Lake**, located just south of Havelock Lake. Snap Lake has been stocked with rainbow trout in the past and can be accessed via the rustic Snap Lake Trail from Stocking Lake Road.

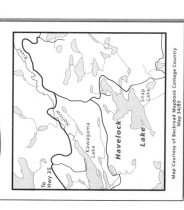

Map Courtesy of Backroad Mapbook Cottage Country Map 34/85

Head Lake

Access

Head Lake forms the western boundary of the scenic town of Haliburton. It is a small, but popular local lake. A public boat launch lies along the southern shore of the lake off Highway 121.

Other Options

There is a number of alternate angling destinations found around the town of Haliburton. In particular, **Jim Beef Lake** is found west of Haliburton off Highway 118. The small lake also offers fishing opportunities for smallmouth bass and the odd muskellunge.

Fishing

Set in the town of Haliburton, Head Lake does see significant angling pressure throughout the season. However, angling success remains decent as visitors can expect fair fishing for smallmouth and largemouth bass and slow fishing for muskellunge.

There is plenty of weed growth located around the lake, especially along the north and eastern ends of the lake. Bass can be found in these weedy areas with subsurface flies and lures. Try working a tube jig or a leech fly pattern in the weed areas for ambush ready bass.

Fishing for musky is inconsistent throughout the summer months, although during the fall musky are often caught in shallow areas, mainly along weed lines. Watch for fishing sanctuary times and locations.

Facilities

The town of Haliburton is a scenic Cottage Country town that is a popular summer destination. The local shops and restaurants are always a buzz from late June to early September. Accommodations are readily available in the area and other facilities such as golfing and established recreation trails help make an ideal outdoor recreation haven.

Lake Definition

Elevation: 324 m (1,080 ft)
Surface Area: 6 ha (15 ac)
Mean Depth: 2.5 m (8.4 ft)
Max Depth: 5.5 m (18.5 ft)
Perimeter: 5 km (3 mi)
Way Point: 45° 03' 00" Lat - N
78° 31' 00" Lon - W

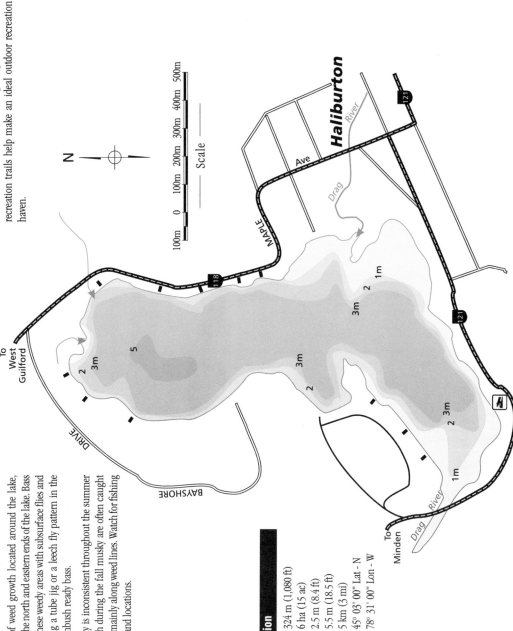

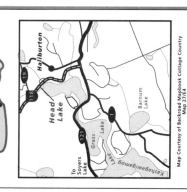

Map Courtesy of Backroad Mapbook Cottage Country Map 27/E4

Horseshoe Lake

Access

Minutes from the town of Minden, Horseshoe Lake can be found via the Horseshoe Lake Road. The Horseshoe Lake Road branches east off Highway 35 just north of the junction with Highway 121.

Other Options

Minden Lake to south and Duck Lake to the north are two angling alternatives near Horseshoe Lake. **Minden Lake** is formed by the damming of the Gull River and is stocked with rainbow trout. Both Minden Lake and **Duck Lake** are home to populations of smallmouth bass. The more remote Duck Lake is often better for smallmouth.

Recent Fish Stocking

Year	Fish Species	Number
2002	Rainbow trout	2,500

Facilities

The town of Minden offers all the necessary amenities for visitors. From groceries to accommodations, visitors should be able to find everything they need to enjoy their stay or visit in the area.

Fishing

Horseshoe Lake is a popular summer destination lake for cottagers and visitors alike. Due to the close proximity of this lake to Highway 35 and the town of Minden, fishing pressure is constant throughout the year. While the angling pressure is heavy, there are some good days out on Horseshoe Lake.

Fishing is fair for largemouth and the odd smallmouth bass in the 0.5-1 kg (1-2 lb) range. Most bass are quite small, although there are a few lunkers caught in Horseshoe Lake each year. The shallow northeast portion of the lake is full of weeds and a good hiding area for largemouth.

A resident population of whitefish also inhabits the lake in decent numbers and are caught by bass anglers on occasion. Using spinners, spoons or flies can target these aggressive fish.

Lake trout and splake were stocked in the lake periodically through the 1980's, but the practice has since stopped. It is thought that there are no more of these trout left in the lake. However, you never know, you may just hook into one since lake trout have been known to live for over twenty years in the region.

Lake Definition

Elevation:	301 m (1,002 ft)
Surface Area:	25 ha (63 ac)
Mean Depth:	7.8 m (26 ft)
Max Depth:	22.5 m (75 ft)
Perimeter:	4 km (3 mi)
Way Point:	45° 01' 00" Lat - N
	78° 39' 00" Lon - W

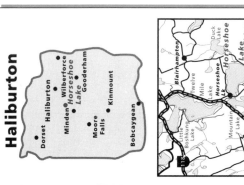

Haliburton

Map Courtesy of Backroad Mapbook Cottage Country Map 27/A5

Johnson Lake

Access

Johnson Lake lies within the Haliburton Forest Reserve. The main entrance to the reserve can be found near the end of Kennisis Lake Road (County Road 7). A road pass, which can be picked up at the permit office, is required to access the lake. They will provide road and/or trail directions into Johnson Lake.

Fishing

Johnson Lake is a very clear lake, which is quite suitable for its resident population of lake trout. Fishing for lakers is best in the winter through the ice, but the early spring can also produce results. A winter hot spot for lakers is the 3 m (10 ft) shoal hump located in the eastern end of the lake. During the winter, lakers will often pass by the shoal in search of oxygen and food.

As the heat of summer approaches, trout head to the depths of the lake and fishing efforts shift towards bass. Largemouth and smallmouth bass inhabit Johnson Lake in fair numbers and can be found along shore structure. Flipping jigs and casting streamers off shore areas can entice bass strikes. The 3 m (10 ft) shoal does attract a number of smallmouth at certain times of the year. Before heading out on Johnson Lake, check your regulations as there are slot size and ice fishing restrictions on this lake.

Other Options

There are several angling alternatives in the vicinity of Johnson Lake. Two of the closer alternatives are **Snap Lake** to the north and **Goodwin Lake** to the west. Snap Lake has been stocked in the past with rainbow trout, while Goodwin Lake has been stocked with lake trout and is also home to a population of smallmouth bass.

Facilities

Facilities around Johnson Lake include a boat access area, designated campsites and a well-developed trail system. Visitors to the forest will also find cabins or rooms in the lodge the perfect way to relax and getaway from it all. Cabins should be reserved prior to arrival. A small fee is required to access and camp at the lake.

Lake Definition

Elevation:	369 m (1,230 ft)
Surface Area:	15 ha (36 ac)
Mean Depth:	17.9 m (59.9 ft)
Max Depth:	44.4 m (148 ft)
Perimeter:	7 km (4 mi)
Way Point:	24° 16' 00" Lat - N
	78° 37' 00" Lon - W

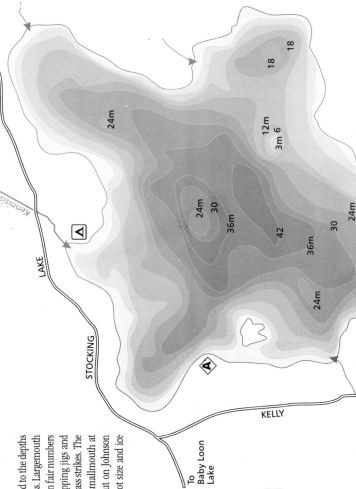

Depth Chart Not Intended for Navigational Use

Scale

100m   0   100m 200m 300m 400m 500m

Map Courtesy of Backroad Mapbook Cottage Country
Map 34/86

Haliburton

Dorset
Johnson Lake
Halliburton
Minden   Wilberforce
          Gooderham
Moore
Falls   Kinmount
Bobcaygean

Kashagawigamog Lake (West)

Access

This long lake is one of the focal points of activity in the Haliburton area. It stretches southwest from the town of Haliburton and has two main access areas found off Highway 121. One launching is located in Haliburton along the northern end of the lake, while the other access is found near the middle of the lake along its northwestern shore. The northern launch is actually located on the small Soyers Lake which is adjoined to the northern end of Kashagawigamog Lake.

Fishing

Kashagawigamog Lake can be a busy spot during the summer months as visitors flock to the area in search of a pleasant rural retreat. Although the lake may be busy, anglers have a variety of sportfish to focus on including bass, lake trout, walleye and muskellunge.

Out of all the species resident in this lake, angling success is best for smallmouth and largemouth bass. Fishing for bass can be good at times for bass that average 1 kg (2 lbs) in size, although they can be found much larger. Weed and rock structure abound around Kashagawigamog Lake making for prime holding areas for bass. Submersible flies and lures are best to find bass; however, these aggressive fish can be enticed to hit top water flies and lures on occasion. The best time to try top water presentations is during overcast periods or in the evening.

Lake trout and walleye are the two most sought after sportfish found in the lake. As a result, the fishing has suffered a bit over recent years. Ice fishing still remains quite popular for both species and ice huts dot the lake in the winter. During the open water season, lakers are best caught by trolling spoons, while walleye can be caught by still jigging. Trolling minnow imitation lures can also produce results for the odd walleye.

A small population of muskellunge also inhabit Kashagawigamog Lake, but fishing is regarded as slow. Some musky anglers will dispute this, and there are reports

of consistent success in the northeast end of the lake at times. The odd musky also hits ice fishing presentations ferociously.

Lake trout slot size restrictions are in place on this lake to help preserve the natural lake trout population. For ice fishing, only one line is permitted to help reduce winter pressure on both lake trout and walleye.

Lake Definition

Elevation: 313 m (1,043 ft)
Surface Area: 81 ha (202 ac)
Mean Depth: 12.7 m (42.5 ft)
Max Depth: 39 m (130 ft)
Perimeter: 34 km (21 mi)
Way Point: 44° 59' 00" Lat - N
78° 36' 00" Lon - W

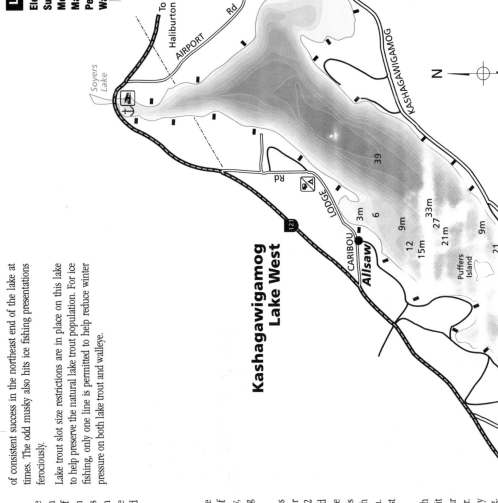

Kashagawigamog Lake West

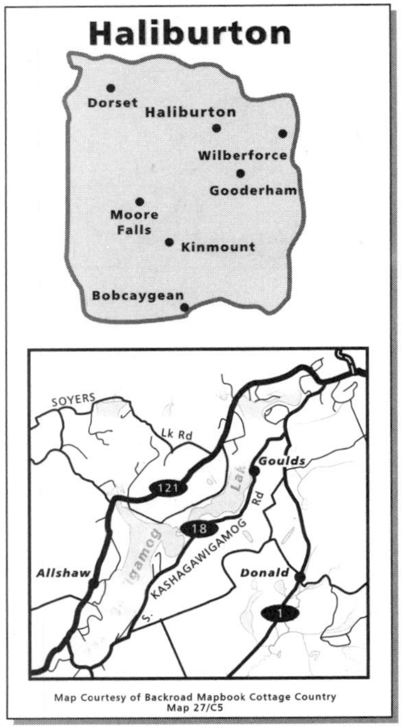

Kashagawigamog Lake (East)

Other Options

If your day on Kashagawigamog Lake is not as successful as you would like, there are several other lakes minutes away that offer additional angling opportunities. **Barnum Lake** is inhabited with smallmouth bass, while **Head Lake** northeast of Kashagawigamog Lake offers fishing for smallmouth bass and the odd muskellunge. Additional nearby lakes include **Soyers Lake, Canning Lake** and **South Lake.**

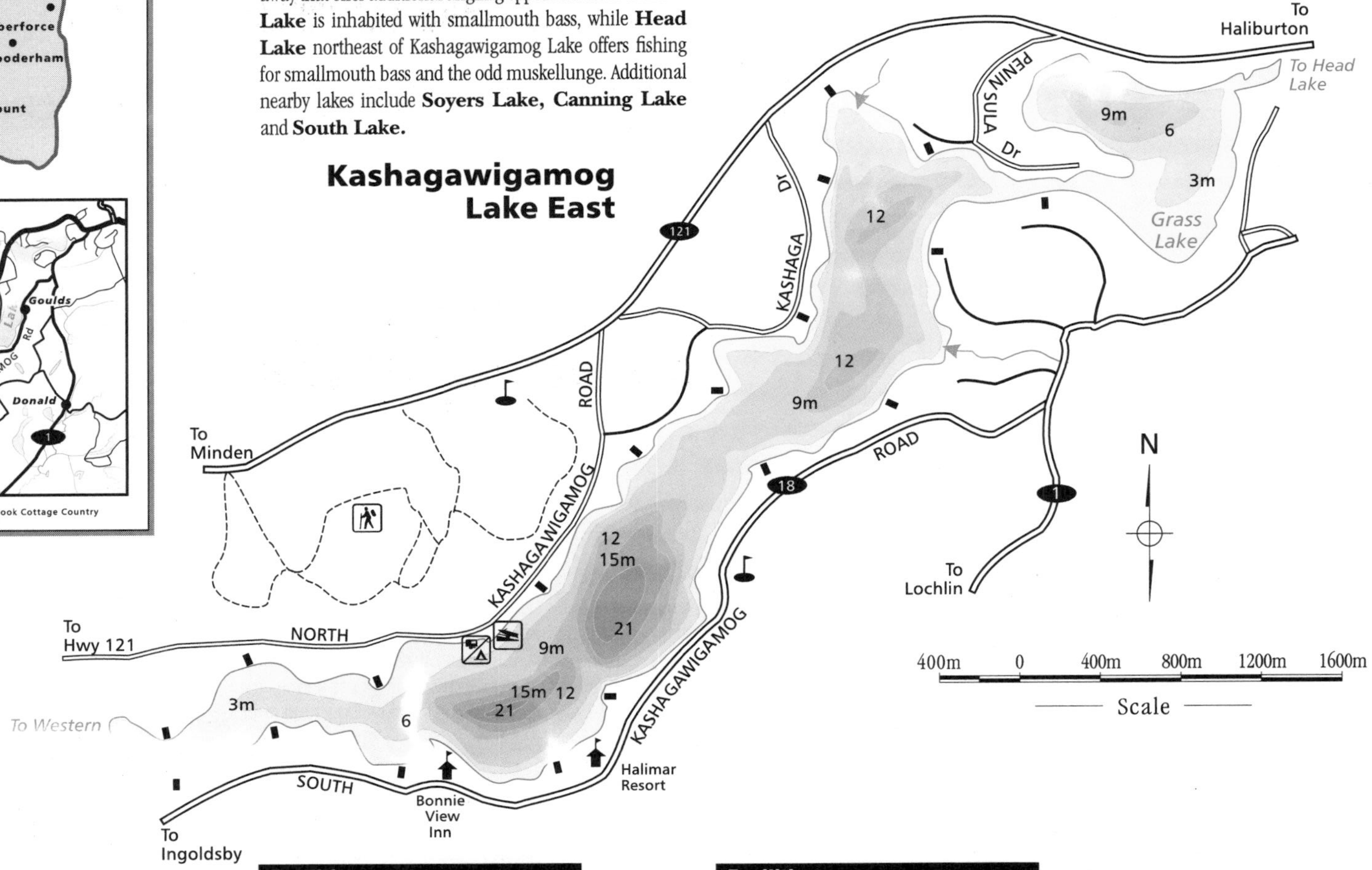

Kashagawigamog Lake East

Facilities

The **Bonnie View Inn** is a small country inn nestled in the trees next to the southeast end of Kashagawigamog Lake. The Inn offers cozy accommodations and gourmet cuisine served in the lakeside dining room. The Bonnie View is open all year providing a remarkable spot for both summer fishing and ice fishing. For reservations call 1-800-461-0347, 705-457-2350 or please visit their website at www.bonnieviewinn.com.

Facilities

Visitors looking for a quiet oasis with charm, warm hospitality and exceptional dining will find the **Halimar Resort** the perfect escape. Set on scenic cascading grounds next to a long sandy beach, the resort provides access to a chain of five lakes. It is a great destination for swimming, fishing, boating, and lots more. For reservations and more information call 1-800-223-7322 or visit www.halimar.com.

Haliburton

- Dorset
- Haliburton
- Wilberforce
- Gooderham
- Moore Falls
- Kinmount
- Bobcaygean

Map Courtesy of Backroad Mapbook Cottage Country
Map 27/C5

Map labels

To Haliburton
To Head Lake
Grass Lake
PENINSULA Dr
9m
6
3m
12
12
9m
KASHAGA Dr
ROAD
To Lochlin
1
18
12
15m
21
9m
15m 12
21
6
3m
KASHAGAWIGAMOG ROAD
NORTH
SOUTH
KASHAGAWIGAMOG
Halimar Resort
Bonnie View Inn
To Minden
To Hwy 121
To Western
To Ingoldsby
121

N

Scale
400m 0 400m 800m 1200m 1600m

Kabakwa Lake

Kabakwa Lake

Access

Kabakwa Lake lies partially within the soutwestern corner of the Leslie M. Frost Centre. Access to the lake can be found via the Shang Ri La Road off Highway 35 north of Carnarvon.

Other Options

If the action is too slow on Kabakwa Lake, you can always venture just south to the Welch Lakes. **Welch Lake** and **Lower Welch Lake** are both inhabited by smallmouth bass, while Lower Welch Lake has been stocked with rainbow trout in the past.

Fishing

Although Kabakwa Lake lies at the southern end of the Leslie M. Frost Centre, it still has a number of camps and cottages along its shoreline. To offset the regular fishing pressure, the lake is stocked regularly with lake trout and has been stocked with rainbow trout in the past. Fishing success can be good at times for both trout species, although catches of rainbow trout seem to be slowing. Ice fishing is productive for trout and success remains steady into the spring.

During the summer months, as trout fishing slows, bass provide the bulk of the action. A fair population of smallmouth bass exists in the lake and bass can be found in the 1.5 kg (3.5 lb) range. Spincasters should try working spinner baits or other attractive lures along shore structure. Fly casters should try working a crayfish pattern close to the bottom for those bigger but often more wary smallmouth.

Facilities

As part of the Leslie M. Frost Centre, there are a few Crown Land, user maintained campsites available on Kabakwa Lake. For more information please call (705) 766-2451 or visit their website at www.frostcentre.on.ca.

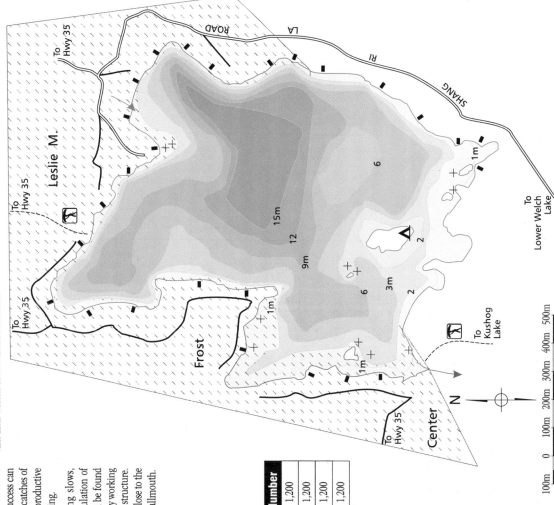

Recent Fish Stocking

Year	Fish Species	Number
2001	Lake trout	1,200
2000	Rainbow trout	1,200
1998	Lake trout	1,200
1998	Rainbow trout	1,200

Lake Definition

Elevation:	366 m (1,220 ft)
Surface Area:	96 ha (238 ac)
Mean Depth:	5.2 m (17 ft)
Max Depth:	19.5 m (64 ft)
Perimeter:	6 km (4 mi)
Way Point:	45° 07' 00" Lat - N
	78° 48' 00" Lon - W

Haliburton

Map Courtesy of Backroad Mapbook Cottage Country Map 26/F2

Kawagama Lake

Access

Kawagama Lake is a large, scenic lake that is not overly busy with boating activity. One of the main and more developed access points is located at Russell Landing. To reach the access, take Highway 35 north from Dorset to County Road 8. Take County Road 8 east and look for signs pointing to the Russell Landing access road. The access road leads to an established boat launch and another car top access area.

Other Options

There are numerous angling options found around Kawagama Lake. A few of the lakes that may be of interest are Herb Lake, Harvey Lake and Bear Lake. **Herb Lake** is a secluded Crown Land lake that is found to the southeast and is inhabited by mainly smallmouth bass and the odd largemouth bass.

Harvey Lake lies to the west of Kawagama Lake and has been stocked in the past with splake. There are also reports of a natural population of brook trout remaining. **Bear Lake** can be found off the northeastern end of Kawagama Lake has been stocked with lake trout in the past. The smaller lake is also home to a population of smallmouth bass.

Fishing

The size of Kawagama Lake can be intimidating to anglers. The key to success for all of its resident sportfish is to locate structure. Work lures and flies in a range of depths in an attempt to find the most productive depth where the bulk of the sportfish are holding.

For the resident smallmouth bass, anglers should focus along the rocky drop-off areas and many weed areas. There are countless quiet bays found around the lake that hold plenty of hungry smallies ready to strike. These bass can also be coaxed to hit the surface at times. Evening periods are your best bet for top water action, although overcast periods can be decent as well.

While smallmouth bass offer the most consistent angling options on Kawagama Lake, many anglers visit Kawagama Lake for its natural population of lake trout. Fishing for these lakers can be fair at times with the bulk of catches coming in the winter during ice fishing season and in the early spring. If you prefer the warmer air of summer, trolling with deep diving equipment such as a Dipsy Diver or downrigger can catch lake trout.

Brook trout once inhabited Kawagama Lake, although the current state of this popular sportfish is unknown. Rainbow trout were also stocked in the lake in the past. Unfortunately, the species is now extinct.

Check the provincial fishing regulations before heading out onto Kawagama Lake, as there are slot size restrictions for lake trout and only one line is permitted when fishing through the ice.

Facilities

Along with the main access area at Russell Landing, there are rough car top access areas at Minden Bay, Fletcher Bay and along the northeast shore off Bear Lake Road. Numerous cottages and camps line the shoreline of Kawagama Lake and may be available for rent. It is best to inquire locally for details. A few resorts are also found in the area. For more information on the Leslie M. Frost Centre, please call (705) 766-2451 or visit their website at www.frostcentre.on.ca

Lake Definition

Mean Depth:	34.3 m (112.8 ft)
Max Depth:	67 m (220 ft)
Way Point:	45° 18' 00" Lat - N
	78° 45' 00" Lon - W

Haliburton

Map Courtesy of Backroad Mapbook Cottage Country
Map 33/F5

Kelly Lake

Access

Located in the Haliburton Forest Reserve, Kelly Lake can be accessed off Kelly Road from North Kennisis Drive. North Kennisis Drive branches off the Kennisis Lake Road (County Road 7) near the Haliburton Forest Reserve front gate. Permits are required to access the lake and can be picked up at the gate.

Other Options

If you are looking for a little seclusion, **Bone Lake** is accessible via 2wd Road to the west. The small lake offers fishing opportunities for decent sized smallmouth bass.

Fishing

Kelly Lake is a remarkably clear lake, with visibility up to 9 m (29 ft). The lake is prime trout water and is inhabited with a natural population of lake trout. These fish provide fair fishing for average sized lake trout. The bulk of the trout action occurs as soon as the season opens in mid May. Trolling with bright coloured spoons or spinners seems to work quite well for the lake trout in Kelly Lake.

During the summer months, lake trout are very difficult to find and fishing is much better for smallmouth bass. Bass found their way into Kelly Lake decades ago and now provide for fair fishing for average sized bass. Anglers should focus their efforts along shore structure, especially off rocky points. In the northeastern end of the lake, there is a rock pile that regularly attracts smallies.

In order to protect lake trout stocks, Kelly Lake is Part of the winter/spring fishing sanctuary period.

Facilities

A cartop boat access point is available along the western shore of Kelly Lake, while rustic hike or boat access camping areas are found on the east side of the lake. For more plush accommodations, the reserve does rent cabins on the lake.

Lake Definition

Elevation: 369 m (1,230 ft)
Surface Area: 10 ha (25 ac)
Mean Depth: 10.8 m (36.2 ft)
Max Depth: 35.1 m (117 ft)
Perimeter: 7 km (4 mi)
Way Point: 45° 15' 00" Lat - N
78° 37' 00" Lon - W

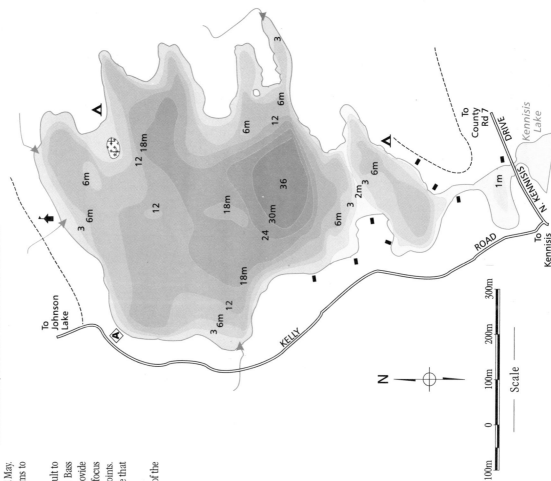

Kennisis Lake

Access

Kennisis Lake is one of the larger lakes in the region and sits in a corner between the Leslie M. Frost Centre and the Haliburton Forest Reserve. From Haliburton, follow Highway 118 west to the Kennisis Lake Road (County Road 7). Kennisis Lake Road leads to the southern shore of the lake where one of the three boat launch areas can be found. The second launch site lies along the northeast end of the lake and an additional access can be found near the northwestern shore of the lake at the Kennisis Lake Dam.

Facilities

Along with the three access areas, there are a number of rental cottages and other privately run accommodations available on the lake. For the adventurous, the Leslie M. Frost Centre to the west of Kennisis Lake is home to numerous backcountry lakes and campsites. To the east, the Haliburton Forest Reserve, a privately organized recreation area, has plenty to offer visitors. At the reserve visitors can camp, rent cabins, stay in a fabulous lodge and explore the many backcountry lakes and trails in the area.

Fishing

Kennisis Lake is a popular summer destination and a number of camps and cottages line the shoreline. The deep lake provides consistent fishing throughout the year for either lake trout or smallmouth bass.

With a maximum depth of 67 metres (223 feet), the lake is an ideal waterbody for lake trout. These naturally reproducing fish provide slow to fair fishing at times for lakers that can reach up to 75 cm (30 in). Ice fishing is quite popular and is perhaps the most successful lake trout angling method on this lake. During the open water season, success drops significantly, although trolling over one of the many mid water humps can produce results.

Sometime in the late 1970s, smallmouth bass found their way into Kennisis Lake and have since established a naturally regenerating population. In general, fishing success is fair for smallmouth bass that average 0.5-1 kg (1-2 lbs) in size and can be found larger. Working shoreline structure is the best method to find smallmouth bass. However, there are reports that at certain times of the year, good numbers of smallmouth congregate around the 7 m (23 ft) shoals that are found around the lake. Be sure to practice catch and release for the preservation of the future sport fishery.

Other Options

Cat Lake and **Blackcat Lake** are two scenic Frost Centre Lakes that can be found via portage from the southwestern shore of Kennisis Lake. Both smaller lakes offer interior rustic camping and are stocked periodically with brook trout.

If you prefer, **Kelly Lake** and **Bone Lake** can be reached by road in the Haliburton Forest Reserve. Bone Lake offers fishing for smallmouth bass, while Kelly Lake is inhabited by both smallmouth bass and lake trout. Road passes are required for access to these lakes and there is a sanctuary period on Kelly Lake to help protect its resident lake trout population. Check the provincial regulations for details.

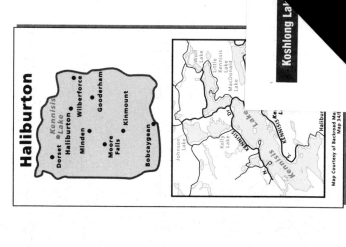

Haliburton

Lake Definition

Elevation:	364 m (1,213 ft)
Surface Area:	140 ha (346 ac)
Mean Depth:	23.1 m (77.1 ft)
Max Depth:	66.9 m (223 ft)
Perimeter:	41 km (26 mi)
Way Point:	45° 13' 00" Lat - N
	78° 38' 00" Lon - W

Depth Chart Not Intended for Navigational Use

Kennisis Lake

Haliburton Forest Reserve

Bone Lake

Paddy Lake

Kennisis Dam

Kennisis River

NORTH DRIVE

KELLY Rd

NORTH

SOUTH

KENNISIS

KENNISIS

KENNISIS LAKE RD

To Hwy 118

To Kelly Lake

Scale

0 400m 800m 1200m 1600m

400m

N

Koshlong Lake

Access

South of Haliburton, Koshlong Lake is accessible by following County Road 1 south to the Koshlong Lake Road. Take the Koshlong Lake Road east and you will soon find a boat launch along the northwestern shore of the lake. Another access point is found a bit further east.

Lake Definition

Elevation:	341.1 m (1,137 ft)
Surface Area:	40 ha (100 ac)
Mean Depth:	10.2 m (34 ft)
Max Depth:	42 m (140 ft)
Perimeter:	11.3 km (7.1 mi)
Way Point:	44° 58' 00" Lat - N
	78° 29' 00" Lon - W

Fishing

Koshlong Lake has had several different names over the years, such as Kokwayong Lake, and Cockweong Lake. The current name was established just after the turn of the 19th Century.

Koshlong Lake was originally inhabited by only smallmouth bass; however, in 1956 the lake was stocked with lake trout. Since the initial stocking was successful, the stocking program has been continued ever since. Fishing for lake trout is quite popular throughout the year and can be fair at times. Ice fishing is one of the more effective methods, but trolling in the spring and fall can be just as productive.

Fishing for smallmouth bass can be good at times for smallies to the 1.5 kg (3.5 lb) range. There is a wealth of bass structure found around the lake, including rock shoals and weeds throughout shoreline areas and in the many shallower bays. In these weedy areas, top water action can be a lot of fun during the evening or on overcast days.

Before fishing, check for special regulations on Koshlong Lake.

Recent Fish Stocking

Year	Fish Species	Number
2002	Lake trout	3,500
2001	Lake trout	2,000
2000	Lake trout	2,000

Facilities

In addition to the access points described above, visitors will find another canoe/small boat access area on the east end of the lake. Accommodations and supplies can be picked up in the town of Haliburton.

If you are looking for a little adventure and some exercise before or after your angling adventure, the Victoria Rail Trail passes to the west of Koshlong Lake and is a great spot for hiking, biking and snowmobiling.

Other Options

If your luck is poor on Koshlong Lake, take a short trip to **Lochlin Lake**. Lochlin Lake can be reached via a rough 2wd road south of Koshlong Lake and offers angling opportunities for smallmouth bass. There is also a boat launch available at the lake.

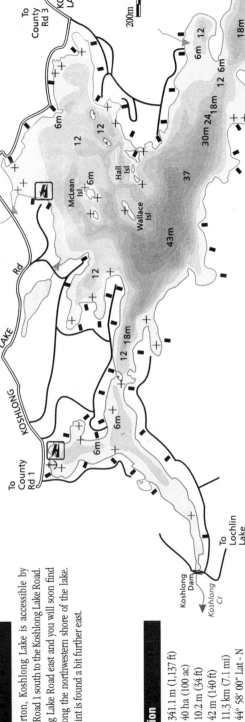

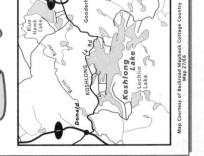

Haliburton

Dorset · Wilberforce · Haliburton · Minden · *Koshlong Lake* · Gooderham · Moore Falls · Kinmount · Bobcaygeon

Map Courtesy of Backroad Mapbook Cottage Country
Map 27/E6

Kushog Lake

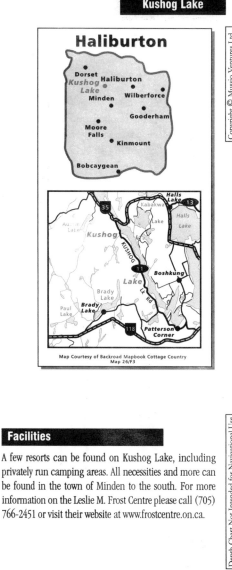

Haliburton

Map Courtesy of Backroad Mapbook Cottage Country
Map 26/F3

Copyright © Mussio Ventures Ltd.

Depth Chart Not Intended for Navigational Use

Access

North of the town of Minden, Highway 35 passes across the narrows at the northern end of Kushog Lake. Access is available near the highway crossing, as well as where the highway skirts the northern end of the lake. Another access point can be found via Buckslide Road at the Buck Slides Dam.

Fishing

Originally, Kushog Lake was named Kakwakshebemahgog Lake, the Ojibway word meaning 'long and narrow'. The tongue-twisting name was later changed to Kushog Lake, most likely for the benefit of English settlers in the area.

Kushog Lake is divided into two different water bodies, the northern arm and the southern arm. The northern arm is dramatically deeper and has a maximum depth of over 30 m (100 ft) compared to 14 m (46 ft) in the southern end. Due to the depth, lake trout tend to be found more regularly in the northern arm. Fishing success for lake trout is usually slow, although is best in the winter through the ice. Slot size and special ice fishing restrictions are in place on the lake to aid the fragile lake trout population.

Anglers looking for consistent action on Kushog Lake are best to fish for its smallmouth bass. Fishing is fair for smallmouth bass up to the 1.5 kg (3.5 lb) range. While smallmouth bass can be found throughout the lake, the southern portion of the lake does offer a little more weed structure for bass to hide in. Try casting spinners, and jigs along rock or weed structures. Fly anglers should try a darker coloured streamer such as a yellow brown leech or wooly bugger.

Other Options

Kabakwa Lake and the Welch Lakes are three lakes located near the northeast end of Kushog Lake. All three are accessible via 2wd roads. **Kabakwa Lake** is stocked periodically with lake trout and hosts a resident population of smallmouth bass. **Welch Lake** and **Lower Welch Lake** are both inhabited by smallmouth bass and Lower Welch Lake has been stocked with rainbow trout in the past, although the species is now extinct from the lake.

Facilities

A few resorts can be found on Kushog Lake, including privately run camping areas. All necessities and more can be found in the town of Minden to the south. For more information on the Leslie M. Frost Centre please call (705) 766-2451 or visit their website at www.frostcentre.on.ca.

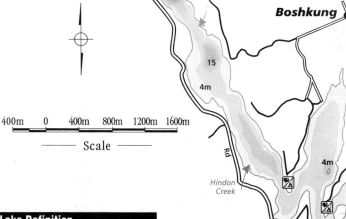

N

400m 0 400m 800m 1200m 1600m

— Scale —

Lake Definition

Elevation:	328 m (1,093 ft)
Surface Area:	58 ha (145 ac)
Mean Depth:	9 m (30 ft)
Max Depth:	36 m (120 ft)
Perimeter:	42 km (26 mi)
Way Point:	45° 04' 00" Lat - N
	78° 47' 00" Lon - W

Haliburton

• Lipsy
• Dorset Lake
• Wilberforce
• Haliburton
• Gooderham
• Minden
• Kinmount
• Moore Falls
• Bobcaygean

To Hwy 118

Little Redstone Lake
Bitter Lake
Tedious Lake
Burdock Lk
Kennisis Lake Rd
Birchy Lake
KENNISIS
Kennisis
Lake S
Lipsy Lake
Wildgoose Lake

Map Courtesy of Backroad Mapbook Cottage Country
Map 27/B1

Lipsy Lake

Access

Lipsy Lake is a secluded backcountry lake that is located south of Kennisis Lake. While there is a road leading south towards Lipsy, it is deemed private. Outside of bushwhacking it in, it is possible to access the lake with a snowmobile in the winter. Please do not trespass.

Other Options

The much larger **Kennisis Lake** has plenty to offer anglers. There are several access points to the lake and fishing opportunities for both lake trout and smallmouth bass.

Fishing

Stocked annually with lake trout, Lipsy Lake provides for fair to good fishing for average sized lakers. Since access is easiest, ice fishing is quite popular on Lipsy Lake and the bulk of the action takes place during this time. For those that can make it in, the action remains consistent just after ice off. Anglers can even catch trout from shore at this time. During the summer, deep trolling is really the only effective angling method that can be used on the lake. Later in the fall, when the water cools, there is a period where trout will come back closer to the surface and are easier to catch.

Facilities

There are no facilities available at Lipsy Lake but rustic Crown Land camping is certainly possible.

Lake Definition

Elevation: 369.9 m (1,233 ft)
Surface Area: 6 ha (15 ac)
Mean Depth: 15.6 m (52 ft)
Max Depth: 46.8 m (156 ft)
Perimeter: 6 km (4 mi)
Way Point: 45° 10' 00" Lat - N
78° 38' 00" Lon - W

Recent Fish Stocking

Year	Fish Species	Number
2002	Lake trout	800
2001	Lake trout	800
1999	Lake trout	800

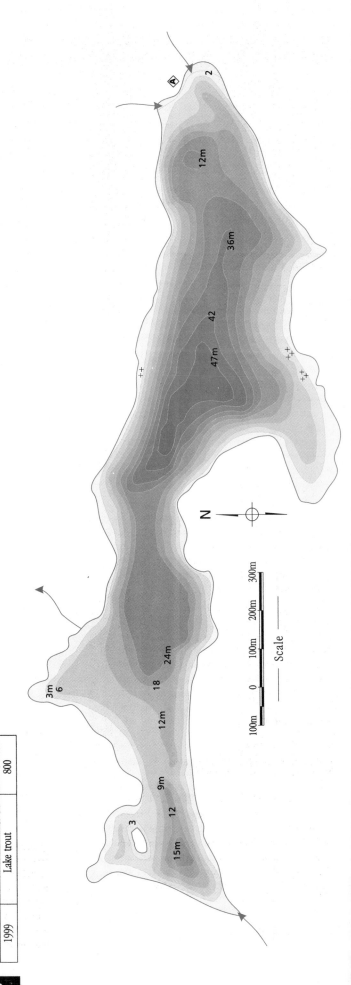

N

Scale

100m 0 100m 200m 300m

Little Bob Lake

Access

To reach Little Bob Lake from Minden, follow Highway 35 north to County Road 2. County Road 2 leads south to Rackety Trail, which branches south to a boat launch at the southern shore of the lake.

Other Options

Right beside Little Bob Lake lays **North Pigeon Lake.** This lake is inhabited with populations of smallmouth and largemouth bass and is stocked annually with lake trout.

Fishing

This small Cottage Country lake is stocked every few years with lake trout. Fishing for these small lake trout is most productive in the spring or by ice fishing in the winter. The northern portion of the lake is often the most productive area for both ice fishing and spring fishing.

During the other times of the year, smallmouth and largemouth bass make up the bulk of the fishing action. Bass average 0.5-1.5 kg (1-3.5 lbs) in size and frequent the shoreline areas. Flipping jigs and spinners along rock walls and other structure can entice aggressive bass strikes. While lake trout seem to be predominantly found in the northern portion of Little Bob Lake, bass can be found throughout the entire lake.

Facilities

In addition to the boat launch, a few private campgrounds are located nearby. Alternatively, visitors can find supplies and roofed accommodations in and around the town of Minden.

Recent Fish Stocking

Year	Fish Species	Number
2001	Lake trout	800
2001	Brook trout	900
2000	Brook trout	900
1999	Lake trout	800
1999	Brook trout	900

Lake Definition

Elevation: 261 m (870 ft)
Surface Area: 6 ha (15 ac)
Mean Depth: 7.8 m (26 ft)
Max Depth: 20.4 m (68 ft)
Perimeter: 8 km (5 mi)
Way Point: 44° 52' 00" Lat - N
78° 47' 00" Lon - W

Haliburton

Map Courtesy of Backroad Mapbook Cottage Country Map 19/F1

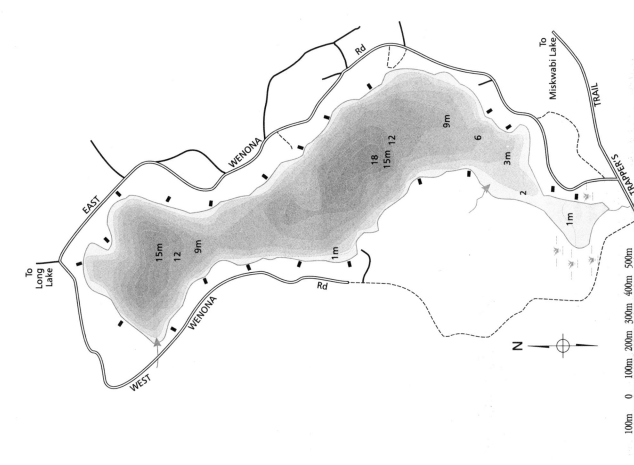

Little Dudman Lake

Access

To reach Little Dudman Lake, follow Highway 121 to the Trappers Trail west of Essonville. The Trappers Trail is a 2wd road that treks north passing by East Wenona Road. This smaller road leads along the east side of the lake. Although there is no formal boat launch, it is possible to hand launch smaller boats onto the lake.

Other Options

If you continue north along the Trappers Trail, you will eventually meet **Miskwabi Lake**. Another fishing alternative is **Long Lake**, which is located due north of Little Dudman Lake. Both lakes have cottages along a good portion of their shoreline and offer fishing opportunities for largemouth bass, smallmouth bass and lake trout.

Fishing

Little Dudman Lake has a number of cottages along its shoreline and receives significant angling pressure throughout the season. While the sport fishery in Little Dudman Lake historically was much better, there remains a population of smallmouth and largemouth bass in the lake.

Fishing for bass is generally fair for average sized bass. Anglers should focus their efforts along shore structure, especially off weedy areas and any rocky outcroppings scattered around the lake. Man-made structures, such as docks, also hold ambush ready bass.

Facilities

There are no public facilities at Little Dudman Lake; however, there are accommodations, retailers and restaurants available in the town of Haliburton minutes away to the west.

Recent Fish Stocking

Year	Fish Species
1999	Rainbow trout
1998	Rainbow trout

Lake Definition

Surface Area: 59 ha (146 ac)
Mean Depth: 6.4 m (21 ft)
Max Depth: 21 m (69 ft)
Way Point: 45° 02' 00" Lat - N
78° 21' 00" Lon - W

Map Courtesy of Backroad Mapbook Cottage Country Map 28/84

Little Esson Lake

Access

Located to the west of Wilberforce, Little Esson Lake can be reached off the Cedar Lake Road, which branches north from County Road 4. County Road 4 travels between the villages of Wilberforce and Essonville and can be picked up off Highway 121. Visitors will find a boat launch along the northern shore of the lake.

In winter, a series of snowmobile trails lead in and around the Esson Lakes.

Facilities

Basic amenities are available in the village of Wilberforce.

Fishing

Rainbow trout used to be stocked periodically in Little Esson Lake. The last stocking occurred in 1999 and the fishing success for trout has curtailed dramatically. It is currently unclear whether rainbow trout will be stocked in the lake again in the future.

For anglers looking for some consistent fishing action, try for smallmouth bass. Smallmouth bass fishing in Little Esson Lake is fair to good at times for bass that average 1 kg (2 lbs) in size. Bass can be found along almost any shoreline structure around the lake. The shallower portions of the lake, especially the western end of the lake can be quite productive. Smallmouth like to hide under weeds and will ambush lures and baitfish. Bass are also common along the steeper middle shoreline areas and around the three small islands found on the lake. Top water lures and flies can be a lot of fun in the evening just before sundown.

Other Options

Three smaller lakes to sample in the area include **Cockle Lake**, **Hillbrow Lake** and **Mountain Lake**. All three lakes have rough road access and fishing pressure tends to be lighter. Anglers visiting these lakes can expect to find fair fishing for smallmouth bass.

Lake Definition

Surface Area:	61 ha (15 ac)
Mean Depth:	7.1 m (23 ft)
Max Depth:	20 m (66 ft)
Way Point:	45° 02' 00" Lat - N
	78° 16' 00" Lon - W

Recent Fish Stocking

Year	Fish Species
1999	Rainbow trout

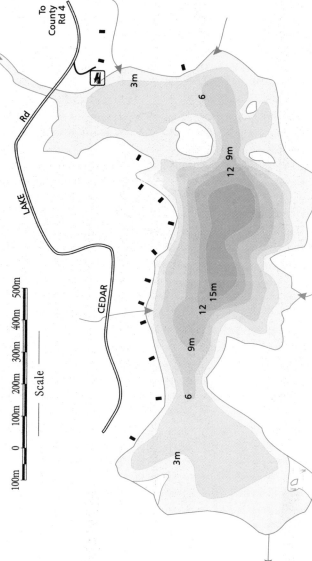

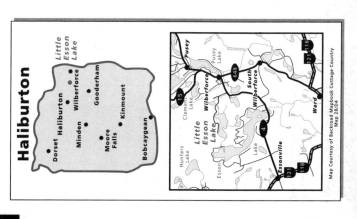

Map Courtesy of Backroad Mapbook Cottage Country Map 28/D4

Little Hawk Lake

Access

Little Hawk Lake lies within the Leslie M. Frost Centre and can be reached via County Road 13. County Road 13 can be picked up off the eastern side of Highway 35 at Halls Lake and leads to the southwestern shore of the lake. A boat launch is available at the community of Little Hawk Lake.

Other Options

If you prefer a more secluded environment, the smaller Cat Lake can be reached via portage from the northeast shore of Little Hawk Lake. **Cat Lake** is home to about six user maintained Crown Land campsites and offers fishing opportunities for stocked brook trout.

Fishing

There are a several camps and cottages on Little Hawk Lake and fishing pressure is constant throughout the year. Similar to most of the deep cool lakes in the Haliburton region, Little Hawk Lake offers primary habitat for lake trout. A natural strain of lake trout inhabits the lake and fishing success is regarded as fair for average sized lakers. Anglers looking to hook into one of Little Hawk's lakers are best to try through the ice in winter. In the spring fishing for trout can still be consistent and is most productive by trolling. With a maximum depth of 87 m (285 ft), it can be hard to locate lake trout in the heat of the summer.

In the summer, smallmouth bass provide the bulk of the fishing action. Fishing can be good for smallmouth bass that average around 1 kg (2 lbs) in size. The far eastern corner of the lake is a consistent producer of smallmouth. The rocky shoreline structure coupled with some underwater rock piles make this a good bass habitat area.

Please practice catch and release to help maintain the natural lake trout fishery.

Lake Definition

Elevation:	354 m (1,180 ft)
Surface Area:	34 ha (85 ac)
Mean Depth:	30.1 m (100.5 ft)
Max Depth:	85.5 m (285 ft)
Perimeter:	20 km (13 mi)
Way Point:	45° 09' 00" Lat - N
	78° 43' 00" Lon - W

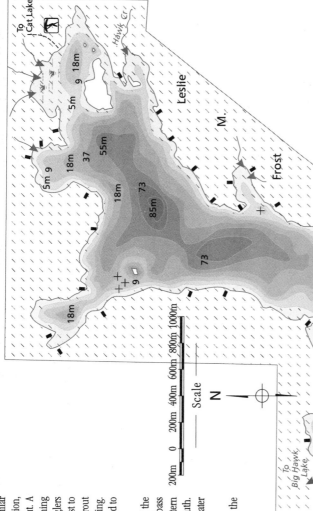

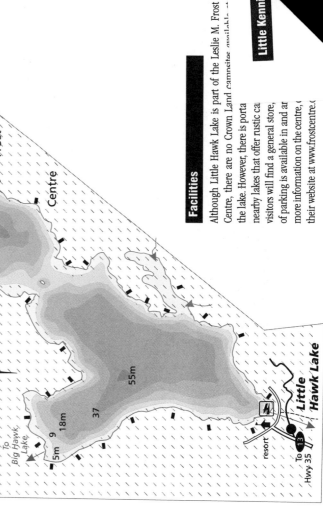

Facilities

Although Little Hawk Lake is part of the Leslie M. Frost Centre, there are no Crown Land campsites available at the lake. However, there is porta... nearby lakes that offer rustic ca... visitors will find a general store, ... of parking is available in and at ... more information on the centre, ... their website at www.frostcentre.c...

Little Kennisis

Leslie

M.

Frost

Centre

To
Cat Lake

Háwk Cr.

Scale

N

200m 0 200m 400m 600m 800m 1000m

To
Big Hawk
Lake

resort

To
Hwy 35

Little
Hawk Lake

Depth Chart Not Intended for Navigational Use

Haliburton

Dorset
Little
Hawk
Lake
Haliburton
Wilberforce
Minden
Gooderham
Moore
Falls
Kinmount
Bobcaygean

Little
Hawk
Lake

Little
Hawk
Lake

BIG HAWK

Halls Lk Rd

Rd 13

Halls
Lake

Buttermilk
Lake

35

HIGHLAND
Rd

Kabakwa
Lake

Map Courtesy of Backroad Mapbook Cottage Country
Map 26/G1

Little Kennisis Lake

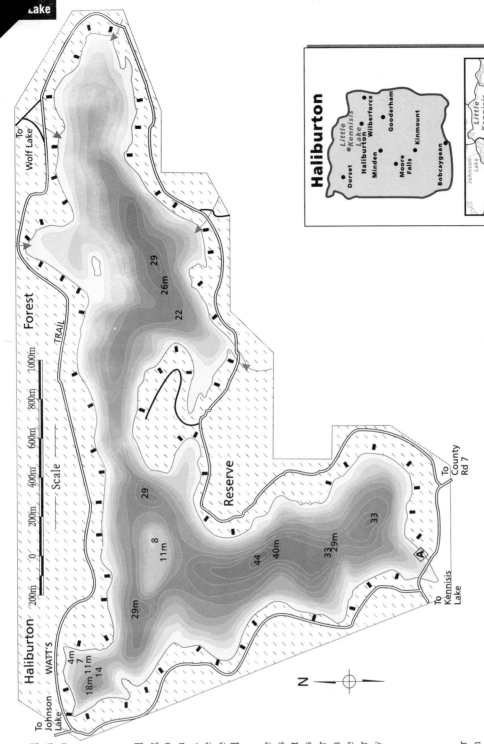

Haliburton

- Dorset
- Haliburton
- Minden
- Wilberforce
- Gooderham
- Moore Falls
- Kinmount
- Bobcaygeon

Little Kennisis Lake
Wolf Lake
Kennisis Lake
To Haliburton
Johnson Lake
Kelly Lake
Kennisis

Scale
200m 0 200m 400m 600m 800m 1000m

To Johnson Lake
To Wolf Lake
Forest
TRAIL
WATT'S
Haliburton
Reserve
To County Rd 7
To Kennisis Lake

4m
7
18m 11m
14
29m
8
11m
29
44
40m
33
29m
33m
22
26m
29

N

Access

To reach Little Kennisis Lake, take the Kennisis Lake Road (County Road 7) north off Highway 118 to the Haliburton Forest Reserve main gate. The gatehouse attendant can direct you to the lake.

Fishing

Little Kennisis Lake is one of the more popular and developed lakes within the Haliburton Forest, although the fishing remains steady. For consistent action, anglers are best to focus their attention on smallmouth bass. Smallmouth provide fair fishing much of the time for average sized bass. In addition to shoreline weed areas and rock structure, the shallow area in the northwest part of the lake seems to be the better fishing areas for smallmouth. Try working jigs and deep running spinners to find these scrappy fish.

A natural population of lake trout also remains in Little Kennisis Lake, and they can reach some nice sizes. Lakers can be found up to 75 cm (30 in) on occasion, but average much smaller. While winter and spring fishing is more productive, open water trolling is the most popular method of angling for these trout. Flashy spoons, trolled in the deeper portions of the lake should increase the chance of hooking into one of these lake trout in the summer months. Please practice catch and release for these highly sought after sportfish.

Facilities

The Haliburton Forest Reserve is a year round outdoor recreation area that includes main lodge and cabin accommodations, a basic general store and rustic camping. Drive-in access camping is available in a number of areas around the reserve. Check out www.haliburtonforest.com for more information on the Haliburton Forest.

Lake Definition

Mean Depth: 18.3 m (60 ft)
Max Depth: 43.9 m (144 ft)
Way Point: 45° 15' 00" Lat - N
78° 36' 00" Lon - W

Other Options

Next to Little Kennisis Lake, **Wolf Lake** and **Dog Lake** are fine alternatives on slow days. Wolf Lake has been stocked with splake and is home to a population of smallmouth bass. Dog Lake is a more remote lake than Wolf Lake and is stocked periodically with brook trout.

Lochlin Lake

Access

To find Lochlin Lake, follow County Road 1 south from Haliburton to the Koshlong Lake Road. Take the Koshlong Lake Road east and after approximately 1 km (0.6 mi) look for a rough 2wd access road to the south. This access road passes the southwestern tip of Koshlong Lake before eventually meeting the northern shore of Lochlin Lake. A cartop boat launch is available at the lake. A high clearance vehicle may be needed in wet weather.

Other Options

If the fishing is too slow on Lochlin Lake, the much larger Koshlong Lake is minutes away. **Koshlong Lake** has two boat launch areas available and provides angling opportunities for lake trout and smallmouth bass. Bass fishing is significantly more productive than fishing for lake trout.

Fishing

This small lake is a beautiful Crown Land lake that is home to a good population of smallmouth bass. The small nature of the lake makes it easy to cover the entire lake in a day. These scrappy smallmouth can literally be found almost anywhere around the lake, although similar to most lakes, shore structure is key. Try flipping jigs or stripping a bulky streamer pattern along the rock piles marked on the depth chart. Unlike some smallmouth lakes, the bass of Lochlin Lake can be very active on the top. For a bit of top water fun, try in the evening or during overcast periods.

Facilities

Lochlin Lake is surrounded by Crown Land and rustic camping is possible. Please pack out any garbage from your campsite.

Lake Definition

Mean Depth: 6 m (19.6 ft)
Max Depth: 9 m (29.5 ft)
Way Point: 44° 57' 00" Lat - N
78° 31' 00" Lon - W

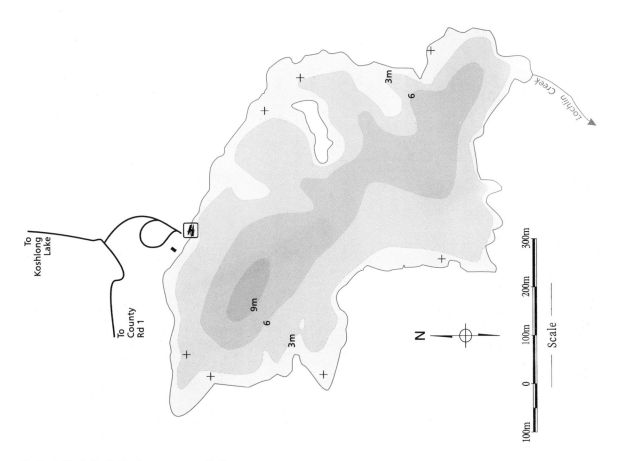

N

Scale

100m   0   100m   200m   300m

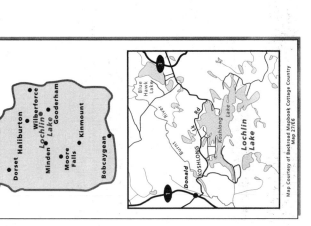

Haliburton

Dorset Haliburton Wilberforce
Minden Lochlin Lake Gooderham
Moore Falls Kinmount
Bobcaygeon

Map Courtesy of Backroad Mapbook Cottage Country
Map 27/46

Long Lake

Access

Long Lake is a popular summer cottage destination found east of Haliburton. Follow Highway 121 east to the East Bay Road and head north. After approximately 2 km (1.2 mi), look for the Long Lake Road. Long Lake Road continues east and follows the northern shore of the lake, culminating at a boat launch area.

Facilities

Other than the boat launch, there are no facilities on Long Lake. The town of Haliburton has plenty to offer travellers.

Fishing

Named Long Lake in 1879, this water body has a long history with bass anglers. Fishing is fair and can be good at times for average sized smallmouth and largemouth bass. Smallmouth are the more dominant fish.

For smallmouth, try working deep water presentations along the rocky shoreline structure around the deeper middle portion of the lake. Lures and flies also produce around the weed structure in the lake. For added fun, bass can often be coaxed to hit surface lures in these weedy areas during the evening. Larger sized fly and poppers are often better for top water action.

Significant populations of largemouth co-exist in Long Lake. Largemouth are predominantly found in the shallower, weedier east and west ends of the lake.

Other Options

En route to Long Lake you will pass by **South Portage Lake.** Smallmouth bass and largemouth bass provide much of the action on the lake, but the odd muskellunge can be found lurking in the shallows.

Lake Definition

Elevation:	382.5 m (1,275 ft)
Surface Area:	88 ha (217 ac)
Mean Depth:	5.3 m (17.9 ft)
Max Depth:	19.5 m (65 ft)
Perimeter:	10.5 km (6.6 mi)
Way Point:	45° 58' 00" Lat - N
	78° 19' 00" Lon - W

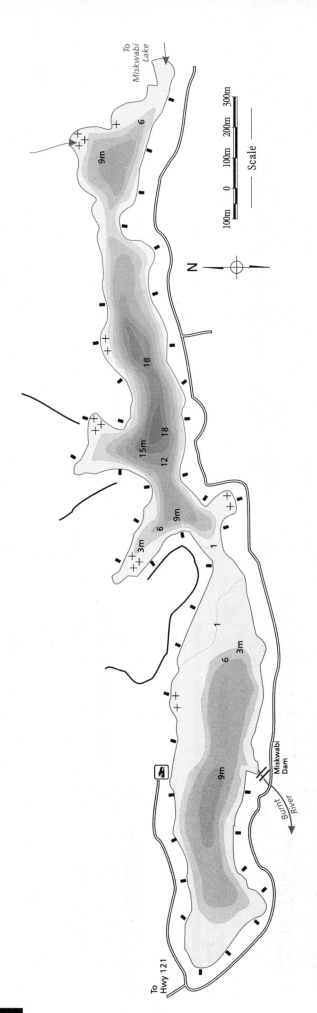

Map Courtesy of Backroad Mapbook Cottage Country
Map 28/A4

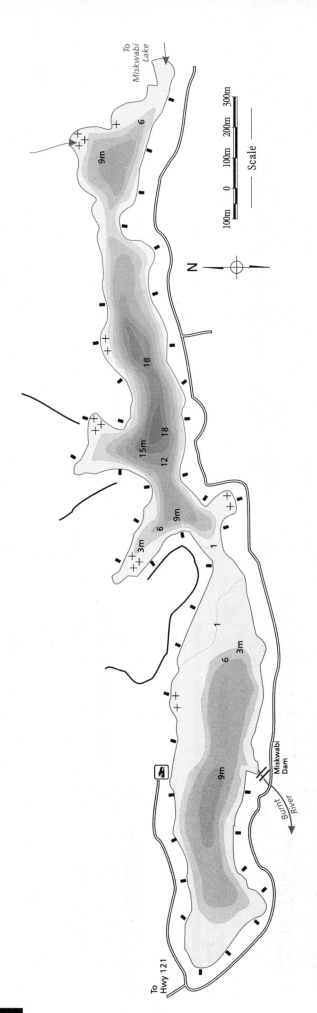

Loon Lake

Access

Loon Lake is accessible off the south side of Highway 121 between the town of Haliburton and the village of Tory Hill. A boat launch is available off Ross Point Road along the southeastern shore of the lake.

Lake Definition

Elevation: 368 m (207 ft)
Surface Area: 242 ha (598 ac)
Mean Depth: 10.8 m (36 ft)
Max Depth: 30.6 m (102 ft)
Way Point: 45° 01' 00" Lat - N
78° 23' 00" Lon - W

Facilities

The nearby town of Haliburton is a scenic Ontario cottage town that has full amenities available. Visitors will find accommodations, retailers and restaurants.

Fishing

The most productive fishing in Loon Lake is for its resident bass. Both smallmouth and largemouth bass can be found in the lake in good numbers and are found exceeding 1.5 kg (3.5 lbs) at times. There is plenty of weed structure found around the lake and fishing is best in these areas. Bass also congregate off Archer Island and Dudman Island.

While fishing success is best for bass, lake trout and walleye are the two most sought after sportfish in the lake. Lake trout are stocked in Loon Lake every few years and provide for fair fishing for lakers that can reach up to 55 cm (22 in) in size. Walleye fishing can be good at times for walleye to 2.5 kg (5.5 lbs). A small population of muskellunge also inhabits the lake.

Ice fishing is a productive time of the season for both lake trout and walleye. Open water anglers will find some of the best fishing of the season just after the spring opening. Walleye are often picked up along weed lines and near the northwest end of the lake. Lake trout are best picked up by trolling along the northern end of the lake and off Archer Island. Muskellunge can be found roaming the shallow bays.

Other Options

West of Loon Lake, **Black Lake** and **Stump Lake** are both accessible off the southern side of Highway 121. Smallmouth bass and muskellunge inhabit the lakes but success is much more consistent for the bass. Due to their close proximity to the highway, both lakes receive significant angling pressure throughout the summer months.

Recent Fish Stocking

Year	Fish Species	Number
2002	Lake trout	1,778
2000	Lake trout	1,778
1998	Lake trout	1,778

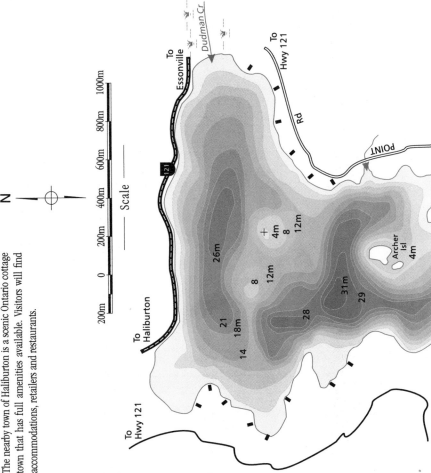

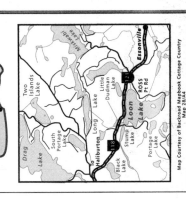

Map Courtesy of Backroad Mapbook Cottage Country Map 28/A4

MacDonald Lake

Access

MacDonald Lake is located on East Road within the Haliburton Forest Reserve. The reserve can be found by following the Kennisis Lake Road (County Road 7) north off Highway 118. Watch for signs directing to the Haliburton Forest Reserve main gate. At the gatehouse ask for detailed directions to the lake.

Other Options

Blue Lake is a much smaller, but more developed lake that is located just south of MacDonald Lake. Blue Lake offers fishing for stocked rainbow trout.

Fishing

A unique natural lake trout population inhabits MacDonald Lake. These lake trout are special because they are only found in nearby Clean Lake and Black Lake. These lake trout are generally smaller than most other Ontario lake trout; however, they seem to be more numerous. Anglers visiting Macdonald Lake can expect fair to good fishing at times for these lakers to 40 cm (16 in) in size. Ice fishing is quite popular and success is consistent through the ice and in the early portion of the open water season. Trollers will find the deeper western end the best area to work later in the year.

Smallmouth and largemouth bass have also found their way into MacDonald Lake and offer good fishing at times for bass that average around 0.5-1 kg (1-2 lbs). Working jigs and spinners along shore structure can be quite good for aggressive bass.

Be sure to check your regulations before fishing on this lake as lake trout have a special season and close early in the year. Please practice catch and release in order to help maintain the unique lake trout and bass species in MacDonald Lake.

Facilities

Set within the Haliburton Forest Reserve, camping and day-use areas are available on the shore of MacDonald Lake. This year round outdoor recreation area also offers a lodge, cottage rentals and a general store. Drive-in access camping is also available in a number of other areas around the reserve. Check out www.haliburtonforest.com for more information on the Haliburton Forest.

Lake Definition

Mean Depth:	17.6 m (58 ft)
Max Depth:	39 m (128 ft)
Way Point:	45° 14' 00" Lat - N
	78° 34' 00" Lon - W

Maple Lake

Access

North of Carnarvon and west of Haliburton, Maple Lake is easily reached via Highway 118. A boat launch is available off Airport Road, which branches north off the highway near the east end of the lake.

Other Options

Just to the north of Maple Lake lies the much smaller **Cameron Lake**. The lake provides fair fishing for smallmouth bass and there are reports of largemouth bass in the lake.

Fishing

Maple Lake is stocked annually with lake trout, which provide for slow to fair fishing at times. This is due in part to the fact that the lake is easily accessed and sees a lot of fishing pressure throughout the year. While lake trout can be found throughout the deeper parts of the lake, the shoal area in the western end is known to attract baitfish and hence, predatory fish like lake trout.

Fishing for bass is generally fair and picks up during overcast periods and in the evening. Both largemouth and smallmouth bass inhabit the lake and average about 1 kg (2 lbs) in size. Bass are best found along shore structure like weed beds as well as near man-made structures like docks.

A population of muskellunge also exists in Maple Lake, although fishing is usually slow.

Facilities

There are a few resorts/lodges scattered around Maple Lake as well as in the immediate area for visitors to enjoy. For supplies and other amenities, the village of Carnarvon and the town of Haliburton are both minutes away from the lake.

Lake Definition

Elevation:	310 m (1,033 ft)
Surface Area:	33 ha (83 ac)
Mean Depth:	11.5 m (38.6 ft)
Max Depth:	37 m (123 ft)
Perimeter:	11 km (7 mi)
Way Point:	45° 06' 00" Lat - N
	78° 40' 00" Lon - W

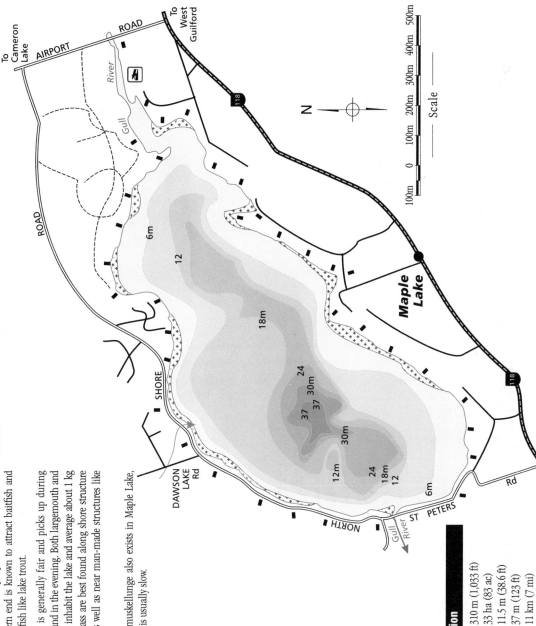

Maple Lake

Haliburton

Map Courtesy of Backroad Mapbook Cottage Country Map 27/42

Minnicock Lake

Access

To find Minnicock Lake, take Highway 121 east from Haliburton to Buckhorn Road (County Road 3). Follow Buckhorn Road south to the Minnicock Lake Road and head east to the southern shore of the lake.

Lake Definition

Elevation:	336 m (1,120 ft)
Surface Area:	6 ha (15 ac)
Mean Depth:	2.7 m (9 ft)
Max Depth:	7.5 m (25 ft)
Perimeter:	6.4 km (4 mi)
Way Point:	45° 00' 00" Lat - N
	78° 24' 00" Lon - W

Fishing

This irregular shaped lake is quite popular throughout the summer and was once home to a population of brook trout. Today, the brook trout are gone, although smallmouth bass fishing has remained steady. Bass anglers have the most success on Minnicock Lake by casting jigs off rocky points and along shoreline structure.

The shallower western end of the lake provides plenty of weed growth, making for prime holding areas for smallmouth. Bass can often be picked up in the deep weeds of the bay, especially during the evening periods of the summer months. When working the weeds, be alert to your line as the area creates many snags. A good way to avoid snags in heavy weed cover like this is to work a weedless spinner bait, a jig or top water lure or fly.

Other Options

Haas Lake lies at the junction of Highway 121 and Buckhorn Road and offers fishing opportunities for smallmouth bass, walleye and the odd muskellunge. A little closer to Minnicock Lake is **Portage Lake**. This smaller lake can be found northeast of Minnicock off of Highway 121 and provides fishing opportunities for smallmouth bass.

Facilities

There are no facilities available on Minnicock Lake.

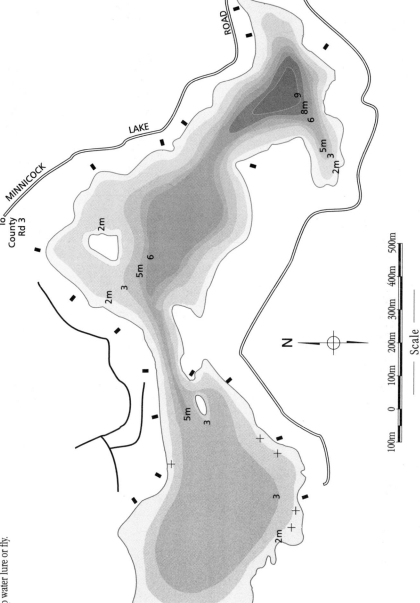

Miskwabi Lake

Access

East of Haliburton, Miskwabi Lake is accessible by following Highway 121 to Trappers Trail. This road heads north to the southwest end of Miskwabi Lake and the public access point. Another access is available to the east via the South Miskwabinish Road.

Facilities

Along with the two access points on Miskwabi Lake, the town of Haliburton and the village of Tory Hill have plenty to offer visitors, including retailers and restaurants.

Recent Fish Stocking

Year	Fish Species	Number
2002	Lake Trout	2,814
2001	Lake Trout	2,800
2000	Lake Trout	2,800

Fishing

Similar to many Haliburton area lakes, Miskwabi Lake is very deep in sections. In portions of the lake, the water level has been recorded at over 43 m (140 ft) deep, making for fantastic summer holding areas for its resident lake trout population. Lake trout were first introduced into Miskwabi Lake in the mid 1960's. Over the past few years, lake trout have been stocked in the lake to supplement existing populations, and success should start to steadily increase over the coming years.

Your best bet to find lake trout is to try during the winter through the ice or in spring just after ice off. Jigging through the ice with a small spoon or lighter colour jig can be effective. During the spring, try trolling a spoon in the upper portion of the lake near drop-off areas and shoals. After summer approaches your best bet for success is to use a downrigger and troll deep for these trout.

Smallmouth and largemouth bass are the more dominant sportfish in this lake and provide for fair to good fishing at times for bass up to 1.5 kg (3.5 lbs). Smallmouth tend to favour the more rocky structure around the lake; therefore, try a jig or crayfish fly off points and other structured areas.

Other Options

Long Lake lies to the west of Miskwabi Lake and can be reached from Miskwabi Lake by boat. Long Lake is best known for its bass fishing as decent populations of smallmouth and largemouth bass exist in the lake. Another nearby angling alternative is **Hunters Lake**. This smaller lake lies to the east and was once stocked with rainbow trout. There are also reports that bass exist in the lake.

Lake Definition

Elevation:	360 m (1,200 ft)
Surface Area:	268 ha (670 ac)
Mean Depth:	18.8 m (62.7 ft)
Max Depth:	43.5 m (145 ft)
Perimeter:	11 km (7 mi)
Way Point:	45° 03' 00" Lat - N
	78° 19' 00" Lon - W

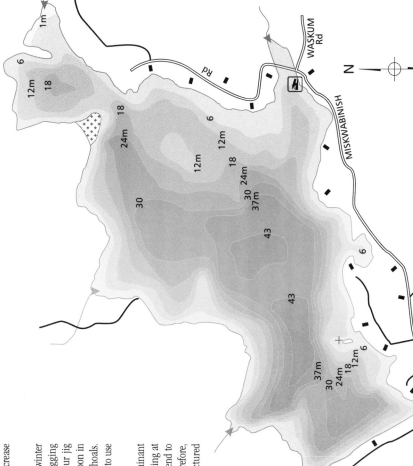

Map Courtesy of Backroad Mapbook Cottage Country
Map 28/83

Monmouth Lake

Access

To find Monmouth Lake, follow Highway 121 east from Tory Hill to Highway 648. This small winding highway leads south to the West Eels Lake Road. The West Eels Lake Road travels west, eventually passing by the southern shore of Monmouth Lake.

Fishing

If you are a bass angler, Monmouth Lake rarely disappoints. There is a good population of smallmouth and largemouth bass available. Bass average 1 kg (2 lbs) in size and frequent the shallow middle of the lake as well as shoreline areas. Smallmouth bass are the main bass species found and are best caught by using deeper water presentations such as streamer flies, jigs and spinners.

Lake trout are stocked in Monmouth Lake annually and provide for good fishing at times for average sized lakers. Ice fishing for lake trout is one of the most popular times of the season to try for lakers. However, in the spring just after ice off can also be productive. Through the ice, try jigging small silver spoons, while trolling spoons is your best bet during the spring.

Lake Definition

Elevation:	329.4 m (1,098 ft)
Surface Area:	7 ha (18 ac)
Mean Depth:	7.5 m (25 ft)
Max Depth:	15.3 m (51 ft)
Perimeter:	5 km (3 mi)
Way Point:	44° 54' 00" Lat - N
	78° 12' 00" Lon - W

Other Options

Right beside Monmouth Lake, visitors will find Lower Monmouth Lake. **Lower Monmouth Lake** is of similar size to Monmouth Lake and offers angling opportunities for smallmouth and largemouth bass.

Facilities

There are no facilities available at Monmouth Lake.

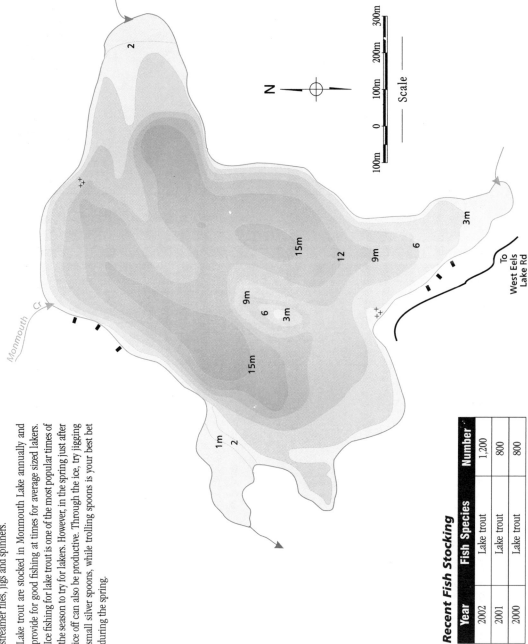

Recent Fish Stocking

Year	Fish Species	Number
2002	Lake trout	1,200
2001	Lake trout	800
2000	Lake trout	800

Haliburton

Dorset · Haliburton · Minden · Wilberforce · Goodergham · Moore Falls · *Monmouth Lake* · Kinmount · Bobcaygean

Map Courtesy of Backroad Mapbook Cottage Country
Map 28/77

Moore Lakes

Haliburton

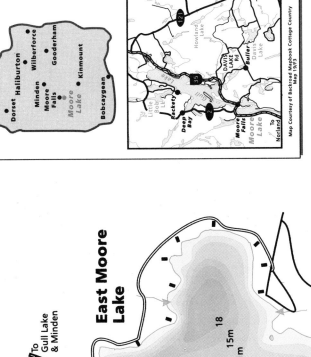

• Dorset   • Haliburton
  • Wilberforce
  • Minden   • Gooderham
    • Moore   • Kinmount
      Falls
         Moore
         Lake   • Bobcaygeon

To
121
Howland
Lake

DAVIS
LAKE
Davis
Buller Lake
Lake
Rd
Gull
35
Lake
Little
Bob
LK
Rackety
Deep
Bay
2
Moore
Falls *Moore*
         Lake
         To
         Norland

Access

Moore Lake and East Moore Lakes are located just north of the village of Norland or south of Minden via Highway 35. The lakes are part of the Gull River system and are accessible via a small marina available in the settlement of Moore Falls.

Fishing

The Moore Lakes can be busy. They are part of the Gull River system, there are cottages scattered around the lakes and they are easily accessed off Highway 35. All of this results in heavier fishing pressure than some of the more out of the way lakes in the area.

The lakes were part of supplemental lake trout stockings in the past, but the resident population of lake trout have been left to naturally reproduce. Success for lake trout is usually slow with the best times being in the winter through the ice or in the early spring just after ice off. In the spring, lakers can be found almost anywhere and can even be caught from shore.

The other main sportfish found in Moore Lakes are smallmouth bass and largemouth bass. Success for both bass can be good on occasion for fish in the 0.5-1 kg (1-2 lb) range. A good area to find largemouth bass is the weedy shallows found around the lakes, especially the region around the outflow and inflow of the Gull River. Try working a top water lure or popper fly for big bucket mouths. Smallmouth bass can be found amid the weedy shallows, although are most predominant off the rocky shoreline areas found around various portions of the lakes.

Be sure to consult your regulations before heading out. Moore Lake has special ice fishing and lake trout regulations in place.

Other Options

Located just outside of Moore falls, **Black Lake** is off the main highway and offers fishing opportunities for smallmouth bass and largemouth bass. Even further north is **Sheldon Lake**. This secluded lake is home to a population of smallmouth bass and is stocked every few years with lake trout. Due to the limited access, fishing should be very good for both species.

Facilities

There is a private campground found south of the lakes. Supplies can be picked up in the village of Norland and near Moore Falls.

Lake Definition

Elevation:	241 m (803 ft)
Surface Area:	117 ha (390 ac)
Mean Depth:	6.9 m (23 ft)
Max Depth:	22 m (73.3 ft)
Perimeter:	11.2 km (7 mi)
Way Point:	44° 48' 00" Lat - N
	78° 48' 00" Lon - W

East Moore Lake

18
15m
11m
7
4m

Moore Lake

Moore
Falls Dam
To
Gull Lake
& Minden
Gull
Lake

7
4m

4m
7
11m
15m
18
22m

4m
7
11m

To
Norland &
Shadow Lake

Black Cr

35

N

Scale
200m 0 200m 400m 600m 800m 1000m

Depth Chart Not Intended for Navigational Use

Moose Lake

Access

Located north of the town of Haliburton, Moose Lake can be reached by taking Eagle Lake Road (County Road 14) north off Highway 121. Just past Eagle Lake, the road passes by the north end of Moose Lake. While a car top boat can be launched at the north end of the lake, the lake is best accessed by boat from Eagle Lake.

Other Options

Blue Lake is found west of Moose Lake and is home to a population of smallmouth bass. Blue Lake is also stocked with splake every few years, which provide for decent ice fishing during winter months. **West Lake** is located south of Moose Lake and is stocked periodically with rainbow trout. A population of smallmouth bass are also resident in the smaller lake.

Fishing

The most active sportfish found in Moose Lake is smallmouth bass. Fishing for smallmouth bass can be good at times for bass that can be found in the 1.5 kg (3.5 lb) range. The rocky nature of Moose Lake provides for plenty of smallmouth habitat. One significant hot spot is the 6 m (20 ft) shoal found near the southeastern portion of the lake. Along this shoal (and other shore structures) jigs can be very effective when worked along bottom areas. Fly anglers should try a crayfish imitation or a good-sized Woolly Bugger to attract big bass.

With shoreline development over the years and the fishing pressure on the lake, it is surprising that lake trout fishing can be fair. The naturally reproducing trout have been able to overcome these obstacles and continue to attract anglers. Ice fishing is a popular winter activity and is one of the best ways to find lakers. During the open water months, trolling is the most effective way of finding lake trout and is best in the spring. If you do happen to hook into a lake trout, be sure to release it unharmed as the species could benefit greatly if catch and release is practised regularly.

Be sure to check your regulations before heading out. Moose Lake has special size and ice fishing restrictions in effect to help preserve lake trout stocks.

Facilities

There are a number of resorts and lodges in the area.

Lake Definition

Elevation: 343 m (1,143 ft)
Surface Area: 29 ha (73 ac)
Mean Depth: 16.3 m (54.5 ft)
Max Depth: 43.2 m (144 ft)
Perimeter: 7.9 km (12.6 mi)
Way Point: 45° 09' 00" Lat - N
78° 28' 00" Lon - W

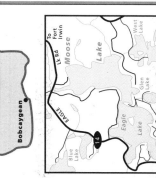

Haliburton

Dorset · Haliburton · Wilberforce · Gooderham · Minden · Moore Falls · Kinmount · Bobcaygeon

Map Courtesy of Backroad Mapbook Cottage Country
Map 27/F1

Mountain Lake

Access

North of the town of Minden, Mountain Lake can be reached by following Highway 35. The highway passes right along the western shore of the lake. The main public access area is found just off the highway on Mountainview Road.

Facilities

There are a number of resorts and lodges available around Mountain Lake. Supplies and all necessities can also be picked up in the town of Minden.

Fishing

This clear lake is quite deep with a maximum depth of over 28 metres (94 feet). A natural strain of lake trout remains in the lake and fishing for these lakers is slow to fair at times. Ice fishing is quite popular and visitors will find numerous ice anglers out on the lake in the winter. Ice fishing also produces catches of whitefish, which make for fine table fare and a decent fight. In the open water months, trolling is the best method of finding lake trout. Since deep-water trolling methods are required for trout in the summer months, anglers should concentrate around the steep eastern shoreline. Trolling here or around the deeper southern hole can be effective.

In the summer months, fishing is best for smallmouth bass. A good population of smallmouth bass exists in the lake for bass that are caught up to 2 kg (4.5 lbs) in size on occasion. Smallmouth can be found throughout the shoreline areas of Mountain Lake, but the inlet and outlet areas of the lake are often more active regions.

Be sure to check the provincial fishing regulations before heading out on Mountain Lake, as there are slot size and ice fishing restrictions in place.

Lake Definition

Elevation:	274 m (920 ft)
Surface Area:	27 ha (68 ac)
Mean Depth:	12 m (40 ft)
Max Depth:	28.2 m (94 ft)
Perimeter:	14 km (9 mi)
Way Point:	44° 59' 00" Lat - N
	78° 43' 10" Lon - W

Other Options

North of Mountain Lake, the small Sharron Lake can be accessed off the east side of Highway 35. **Sharron Lake** is often overlooked by passersby but is home to a population of feisty smallmouth bass.

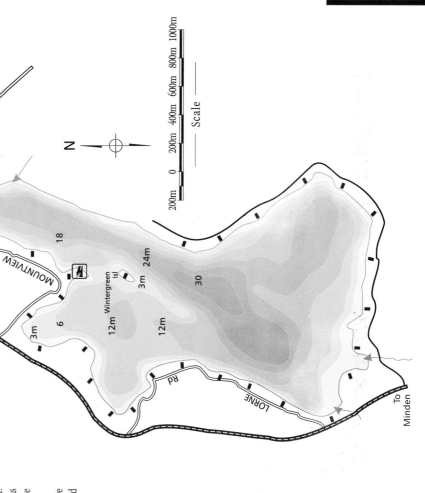

Map Courtesy of Backroad Mapbook Cottage Country
Map 27/A6

North Lake

Access

To find North Lake follow the Harburn Road (County Road 19) north from the town of Haliburton to the settlement of Fort Irwin. Continue north from Fort Irwin past the Ross Lake Road and look for the North Lake Road, which leads directly to North Lake. Please do not trespass.

Facilities

There are no facilities available at North Lake.

Fishing

North Lake is a secluded lake that receives marginal angling pressure throughout the year. Fishing in the lake is best during the summer months for its resident smallmouth bass. Bass fishing is often fair for smallmouth bass that average 0.5-1 kg (1-2 lbs) in size. While shoreline structure creates some activity for bass, the two shallow shoal areas found in the lake are often a better area to fish for smallmouth. At certain times of the season the 7 m (24 ft) shoal hump found in the western end of the lake hold a significant number of smallmouth. Anglers should try deep water tactics to hook into these shoal area smallies.

A natural population of lake trout also remains in North Lake, although fishing is usually slow. Spring fishing can be exciting, although it more often results in hours of casting and trolling. If you do hook into one of these natural lakers, catch and release can go a long way to help sustain this natural trout species. North Lake is part of the winter/spring fish sanctuary period to help sustain its natural lake trout population.

Other Options

Northeast of North Lake, visitors can find **East Lake** via the East Lake Road. The lake is rumoured to have a self-sustaining population of brook trout. Another alternative is **Martin Lake,** which is accessed by an ATV trail north of East Lake. Martin Lake is stocked every few years with brook trout.

Lake Definition

Elevation:	392.3 m (1,287 ft)
Surface Area:	74 ha (182 ac)
Mean Depth:	14 m (46 ft)
Max Depth:	37 m (121 ft)
Perimeter:	5 km (3 mi)
Way Point:	45° 15' 00" Lat - N
	78° 24' 00" Lon - W

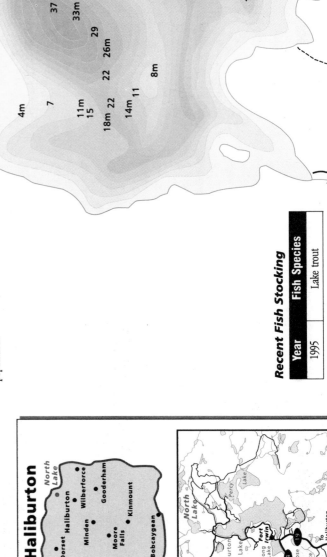

Recent Fish Stocking

Year	Fish Species
1995	Lake trout

Haliburton

North Lake

Dorset   Haliburton
Minden   Wilberforce
         Gooderham
Moore
Falls   Kinmount
         Bobcaygeon

North Lake

To Haliburton Lake

Haliburton Lake   Percy Lake

Oblong Lake   Fort Irwin   19

14   Moose Lake   Haliburton

Map Courtesy of Backroad Mapbook Cottage Country Map 34/56

Nunikani Lake

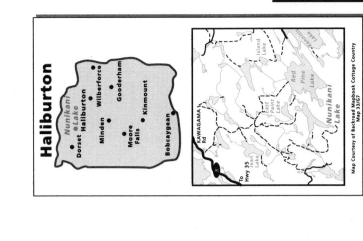

Haliburton

Map Courtesy of Backroad Mapbook Cottage Country
Map 33/G7

Copyright © Mussio Ventures Ltd.

Depth Chart Not Intended for Navigational Use

Access

Nunikani Lake lies within the fabulous Leslie M. Frost Centre. This scenic backcountry lake is only accessible by canoe and portage from Red Pine Lake to the east or Big Hawk Lake to the south.

Fishing

Nunikani Lake is a deep greenish coloured lake that experiences limited angling pressure throughout the year. As a result, the lake provides good fishing for bass that average around 0.5 kg (1 lb) in size. Smallmouth bass are the dominant species, but there are reports that largemouth bass can also be caught in the lake. Bass frequent the shoreline areas of the lake, although deep holding bass can also be found along the 6 m (20 ft) shoal located near the middle of the lake.

Similar to most of the deep rocky lakes in the region, Nunikani Lake also hosts a population of lake trout. The natural strain of lake trout can be found up to 65 cm (26 in) in size, although average much smaller. Ice fishing can provide results during the winter months, although the best time to visit Nunikani Lake for lake trout is in the spring just after ice off. As the heat of summer sets in, the lakers of Nunikani Lake become very challenging to find as they revert to the depths of the lake.

To help preserve the natural strain of lake trout please practice catch and release. Special regulations such as slot size restrictions and ice fishing restrictions are in place on this lake. Be sure to check provincial regulations before fishing.

Other Options

Red Pine Lake is a good-sized lake that can be found by portage from the northeastern end of Nunikani Lake. Similar to Nunikani Lake, anglers can expect to find smallmouth bass and a natural strain of lake trout in Red Pine Lake. Portions of the bigger lake are part of the Leslie M. Frost Centre and rustic campsites have been established. There are also a few camps and cottages on parts of the lake.

Facilities

The Leslie M. Frost Centre is an Ontario Ministry of Natural Resources training area. The property is open to the public and contains numerous secluded lakes that can be accessed by trail, road or portage. Crown Land campsites can be found along most lakes in the centre including at Nunikani Lake. Currently there is no fee for usage, although the centre is quite busy during the months of July and August. To contact the centre, please call (705) 766-2451 or visit their website at www.frostcentre.on.ca.

Lake Definition

Elevation:	371 m (1,237 ft)
Surface Area:	11 ha (28 ac)
Mean Depth:	7.7 m (25.9 ft)
Max Depth:	23.7 m (79 ft)
Perimeter:	11 km (7 mi)
Way Point:	45° 12' 00" Lat - N
	78° 44' 00" Lon - W

Kennisis River

Leslie M.

Frost

Center

Nunikani Dam

N

Scale

100m 0 100m 200m 300m 400m 500m

Oblong Lake

Access

Northeast of Haliburton, Oblong Lake can be reached by following the Haliburton Lake Road (County Road 19) north to the junction with County Road 14. County Road 14 continues west along the south side of the lake, while the Haliburton Lake Road continues north to the settlement of Fort Irwin. A boat launch area is found off the Haliburton Lake Road.

Fishing

Oblong Lake is a popular summer destination lake and receives significant angling pressure throughout the year. A dam found along the southwestern end of the lake also affects the fishing. The dam helps regulate the water levels of the Trent Canal system to the south and can fluctuate the water level in the lake by over 2 m (6.5 ft). These water fluctuations can affect fishing quality, especially if there is a rapid change in the level from day to day.

Anglers visiting Oblong Lake will find a fair population of smallmouth bass in the 0.5-1 kg (1-2 lb) range. There is plenty of weed and rock structure found along the shoreline areas of the lake. While bass can be enticed to hit top water flies and lures at times, the best method of finding these smallmouth is with deeper water presentations near the cover. Spinners and tube jigs can work well, as can streamer type flies.

A natural population of lake trout also remains in Oblong Lake. Fishing is generally slow for lakers that are quite small. The lake is protected by the winter/spring fishing sanctuary and it is recommended to practice catch and release to help maintain this fragile indigenous species.

Other Options

North of Oblong Lake, the Harburn Lakes can be found. **Harburn Lake** and **Little Harburn Lake** are two remote access lakes that are stocked every few years with brook trout. Ice fishing can be quite good, while the spring is another productive time of year.

Facilities

Outside of the boat launch area, there are few facilities for visitors on Oblong Lake. The town of Haliburton is minutes away to the south and has plenty to offer visitors to the Haliburton area.

Lake Definition

Elevation: 356 m (1,187 ft)
Surface Area: 9 ha (22 ac)
Mean Depth: 9.8 m (32.8 ft)
Max Depth: 27 m (90 ft)
Perimeter: 5 km (3 mi)
Way Point: 45° 11' 00" Lat - N
78° 26' 00" Lon - W

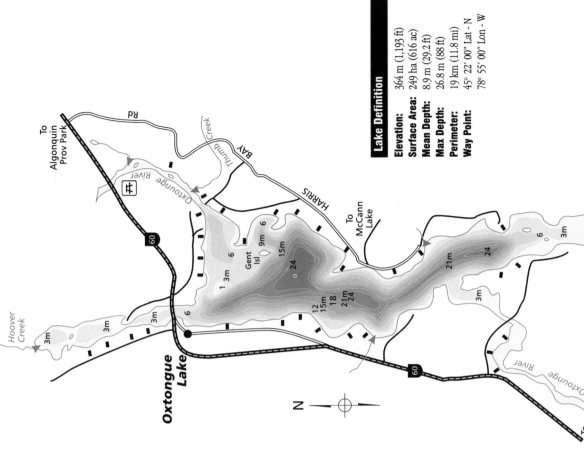

Lake Definition

Elevation:	364 m (1,193 ft)
Surface Area:	249 ha (616 ac)
Mean Depth:	8.9 m (29.2 ft)
Max Depth:	26.8 m (88 ft)
Perimeter:	19 km (11.8 mi)
Way Point:	45° 22' 00" Lat - N
	78° 55' 00" Lon - W

Scale

Oxtongue Lake

Access

Oxtongue Lake is located just outside of Algonquin Provincial Park and can be reached off the south side of Highway 60. There are a number of access points to the lake including the option of launching a canoe from the side of the highway

Other Options

Across Highway 60 north of Oxtongue Lake, anglers can find the remote access **Beetle Lake** and **Martencamp Lake.** The lakes have been stocked in the past with brook trout and are both scenic, secluded Algonquin area lakes.

Fishing

Oxtongue Lake has a long history as it was an intrigal part of the first log drives in the area. Today, it is a popular year round retreat that offers trout and bass fishing.

Oxtongue Lake was once a notable trout destination. In addition to a natural population of brook trout, rainbow trout were stocked in the lake. Both species are now extinct, but there is the odd report each year that brook trout have been caught. It is thought that they are most likely misidentified lake trout.

A natural strain of lake trout remains and they provide fair fishing on occasion. Ice fishing is probably the best way to find these lake trout; however, trolling in the spring is also a popular method. In order to protect the natural strain of lake trout in Oxtongue Lake, slot size and special ice fishing restrictions have been established.

Thirty years ago, smallmouth bass were a rarity in Oxtongue Lake. Today, similar to many lakes in Ontario, smallmouth bass have become a major part of the ecosystem and a popular sport fishing alternative. Smallmouth in Oxtongue Lake average around 1 kg (2 lbs) in size and can often be found around the inflow of the Oxtongue River. The small island and the 2 metre (7.5 foot) shoal in this area are two of the better holding areas for bass. Try working jigs and streamer type flies along these structures.

Facilities

Several resorts, motels and other accommodations are established in and around Oxtongue Lake. There is also a picnic site next to the river at the northeast end of the lake. For visitors looking to camp in the area, nearby Algonquin Park is a fantastic place to visit throughout the year. Supplies and other amenities can be found in the town of Huntsville to the west and the village of Dorset to the south.

Haliburton

Oxtongue Lake
Dorset
Haliburton
Minden
Wilberforce
Gooderham
Moore Falls
Kinmount
Bobcaygeon

Beetle Lake
Oxtongue Lake
To Algonquin Prov Park
Notsobig Lake
HARRIS BAY Rd
Oxtongue Lake
McCann Lake
Feline Lake
Sixteen Mile Lake
60
To Huntsville

Map Courtesy of Backroad Mapbook Cottage Country Map 33/B3

Percy Lake

Access

Currently, there is no public right of way into Percy Lake. While there are roads around the lake, they are private and off limits to the public. Short of asking permission to use one of the roads in the area, Percy Lake can be accessed via a short 600 m (1,973 ft) portage from Haliburton Lake. The portage is not well used, but can be found by locating the inflow of the Gull River into Haliburton Lake.

Other Options

North Lake lies just to the northwest of Percy Lake and was stocked at one time with lake trout. The lake now relies on natural reproduction to maintain the lake trout fishery. Smallmouth bass also inhabit the lake. Check the regulations before fishing this lake, as it is part of the winter/spring fishing sanctuary.

Lake Definition

Elevation:	375 m (1,250 ft)
Surface Area:	34 ha (85 ac)
Mean Depth:	10.8 m (36 ft)
Max Depth:	33 m (110 ft)
Perimeter:	23 km (14 mi)
Way Point:	45° 12' 00" Lat - N
	78° 22' 00" Lon - W

Fishing

Percy Lake was named after an official of the historic Canada Land and Emigration Company. In the mid 1800's, the British company was a major player in helping develop the Haliburton area through the development and sale of land parcels in the region.

Visitors to Percy Lake can expect to find a beautiful Haliburton Lake with a few cottages and camps along its shoreline. Beginning as far back as 1964, Percy Lake has been stocked every few years with lake trout. Angling success for lake trout is usually fair for trout that can be found up to 75 cm (30 in) in size on occasion. Ice fishing provides consistent results each year, while trolling is the best method of catching lakers during the open ice season.

Despite the lake trout, it is the resident smallmouth bass that provide the bulk of the fishing action on the lake. Fishing can be good for smallmouth, especially during dusk or overcast periods. From rocky shoreline areas to the massive weed bed found in the eastern part of the lake, there is ample habitat for this aggressive fish. Both top water and submersible angling techniques can produce results in this lake. Bass have been known to reach up to 2 kg (4.5 lbs) in size, but average much smaller.

All anglers visiting Percy Lake must take into account the small dam on the western end of the lake. The dam helps regulate the water levels of the Trent Canal system to the south and can fluctuate the lake level by over 2 m (6.5 ft). Water fluctuations can affect fishing quality, especially if there is a rapid change in the level from day to day.

Facilities

While there are a few cottages on the shore of Percy Lake, there are no public facilities available at the lake.

Recent Fish Stocking

Year	Fish Species	Number
2002	Lake Trout	5,100
1998	Lake Trout	5,100
1996	Lake Trout	5,100

82

Pusey Lake

Access

Pusey Lake is a long lake that lies near the settlement of Wilberforce along Highway 648. The lake can be found by following Highway 121 east to the smaller Highway 648. The 648 snakes north, eventually passing by the western shore of Pusey Lake and the public boat launch at the southern end of the lake.

Other Options

Just to the west of Pusey Lake, visitors can find two decent angling alternatives to Pusey Lake. **Clement Lake** and **Little Esson Lake** have been stocked in the past with rainbow trout and offer decent fishing opportunities for smallmouth bass. Both lakes have boat launch areas to aid anglers.

Facilities

In addition to the boat launch and picnic area, there are a few resorts and a campsite located on Pusey Lake.

Fishing

A small dam found along its southern shore regulates the water level of Pusey Lake. The dam is part of a vast array of dams in place to regulate water levels on the Trent Canal to the south. While water levels do fluctuate, the fluctuations are minimal and rarely affect the fishing quality of the lake.

Fishing success in Pusey Lake is best for its resident smallmouth bass. Bass can be found almost anywhere along the shoreline of the lake, with spinners and jigs producing results regularly. The inflow of a small creek located in the northeastern end of the lake tends to have decent weed cover for smallmouth bass. Another prime area to find smallmouth is in the middle of the lake where the lake is separated by a shallow area. Bass can find plenty of cover in this area, which is best worked with weedless type presentations.

In the spring you may get lucky and hook into one of Pusey Lake's natural lake trout. Although fishing success for lakers is usually slow, anglers do catch them during the first few weeks of the season. Trout are occasionally caught in the southern, shallower end of the lake, but the vast majority of catches are experienced in the deeper, northern end of the lake.

Trolling a flashy silver or gold spoon is the best way to find open water lake trout. In the summer, these lakers, like in most lakes, will revert to the depths of the lake in search of cooler waters. During this time, the only way to catch a lake trout is by using downrigging equipment. Special slot size and winter ice fishing regulations are in place on this lake to help sustain the natural lake trout population. Please practice catch and release whenever possible for these fragile species.

Lake Definition

Elevation:	378 m (1,260 ft)
Surface Area:	5 ha (13 ac)
Mean Depth:	9.9 m (33.2 ft)
Max Depth:	37.5 m (125 ft)
Perimeter:	6 km (4 mi)
Way Point:	45° 03' 00" Lat - N
	78° 13' 00" Lon - W

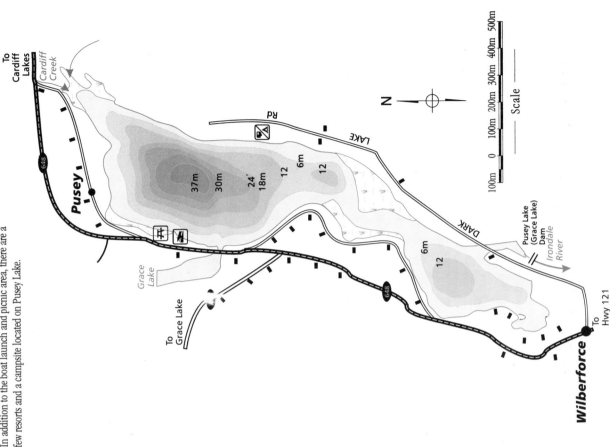

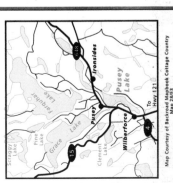

Map Courtesy of Backroad Mapbook Cottage Country Map 28/63

Raven Lake

Access

South of the village of Dorset there is a public boat launch area off Highway 35 along the westernmost arm of Raven Lake. The launching site is quite busy during the summer months, although there is plenty of parking available.

For an alternate access to Raven Lake, follow County Road 8 east off Highway 35. There is an access road found west of Minden off Highway 35. The road branches south off County Road 8 and leads to the northeastern arm of Raven Lake.

Facilities

Raven Lake is part of the Gun Lake Canoe Route. In addition to the two access points, there are rustic interior campsites available for self-sufficient campers. For more information on the centre, please call (705) 766-2451 or visit www.frostcentre.on.ca.

Fishing

Due to the close proximity of Raven Lake to Highway 35 and the village of Dorset, Raven Lake receives significant angling pressure throughout the year. At times during the summer the public launch area of the highway is packed with cars and boat trailers. Fishing in the lake is best during the summer months for its resident smallmouth bass, earlier and later in the year, lake trout are the main target of anglers.

Bass fishing is regarded as fair for smallmouth bass that can reach up to 2.5 kg (4.5 lbs) in size but average 0.5-1 kg (1-2 lbs). There are numerous back bays with rocky shoreline structure where smallmouth are often found. Anglers should also try working lures and flies along any of the small islands around the lake. Spinner baits or tube jigs are the lures of choice for Spincasters. Fly anglers using a crayfish imitation fly off bottom areas often out fish their spincasting counterparts.

Fishing is often slow for the natural population of lake trout that remains in North Lake. Anglers will find more success by trolling spoons in the spring. To help maintain this natural lake trout population, slot size restrictions are in place for lake trout and only one line is permitted for use during ice fishing. Check the provincial fishing regulations for details.

Other Options

Anglers looking for a secluded fishing lake should try Gun Lake to the east of Raven Lake. **Gun Lake** is accessible via a 360 m (1,181 ft) portage and offers rustic interior camping opportunities. The lake is inhabited by both smallmouth and largemouth bass.

Lake Definition

Elevation:	344 m (1,147 ft)
Surface Area:	55 ha (138 ac)
Mean Depth:	8.0 m (26.7 ft)
Max Depth:	41.1 m (137 ft)
Perimeter:	36 km (23 mi)
Way Point:	45° 12' 00" Lat - N
	78° 51' 00" Lon - W

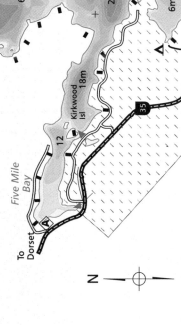

Haliburton

Dorset · Raven Lake · Haliburton · Minden · Wilberforce · Gooderham · Moore Falls · Kinmount · Bobcaygeon

Map Courtesy of Backroad Mapbook Cottage Country Map 33/07

Red Pine Lake

Access

This semi-secluded lake is part of the Leslie M. Frost Centre and is accessible by boat from along the Kennisis River. To reach the boat launch on the Kennisis River, follow the Kennisis Lake Road (County Road 7) north off Highway 118 to North Kennisis Drive. This access road wraps around the northern end of Kennisis Lake, eventually ending at the access point below the Kennisis Lake Dam. You can launch a boat or canoe into the river and proceed west for approximately 2 km (1.2 mi) to the southeastern end of Red Pine Lake.

Facilities

At the Kennisis Lake Dam access point, visitors will find a well established boat launching area complete with toilets and parking. Red Pine Lake is part of the Leslie M. Frost Centre and much of the lake remains Crown Land. Seven user maintained campsites are available on the lake, including a few very picturesque island sites. If you do plan to camp, be sure to carry out any garbage from your campsite. For more information on the centre, please call (705) 766-2451 or visit www.frostcentre.on.ca.

Other Options

In the northeast arm of Red Pine Lake, ambitious anglers will find a 1,300 m (4,265 ft) portage north into a lake named East Paint Lake. **East Paint Lake** is a beautiful, secluded Frost Centre Lake that is mainly visited in the winter by snowmobilers. The lake is stocked every few years with splake and is home to a nice backcountry campsite.

Fishing

With the limited access to Red Pine Lake, the lake does not receive as much angling pressure as other lakes in the area. The bulk of the angling pressure comes from the summer cottage residents on the lake and some of the canoe trippers that venture into the lake throughout the summer.

Red Pine Lake is a very clear lake that is inhabited with smallmouth bass and a naturally reproducing strain of lake trout. The lake has many islands and is home to numerous back bays, which provide good holding areas for bass. Look for smallmouth near rocky shoreline structures or shoal areas in the 3 m (10 ft) range. Bass average about 0.5 kg (1 lb) in size, although are caught larger on occasion in Red Pine Lake. Smallmouth will often strike lures and flies like spinners or streamers. When fishing success is slow, try flipping a jig or crayfish imitation off the bottom.

Similar to most lakes in the region, the most sought after sportfish in Red Pine is lake trout. Fishing for lakers is usually slow, although it can be fair at times in the winter or in the spring, just after ice off. The trout in this lake are a naturally reproducing strain; therefore, if you do happen to catch one of these fragile species, please practice catch and release. Watch for special regulations.

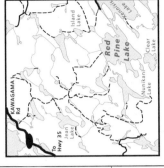

Haliburton

Dorset •   Red Pine   • Wilberforce
  Lake
Minden • Haliburton •   • Gooderham
  Moore
  Falls • Kinmount
  • Bobcaygeon

KAWAGAMA Rd
To Hwy 35
Jean Lake
Nunikani Lake
Clear Lake
Red Pine Lake
Island Lake
Kennisis Lake

Map Courtesy of Backroad Mapbook Cottage Country
Map 33/G7

Leslie M.

To East Paint Lake

To Nupikani Lake

Kennisis River

Frost Centre

Haliburton Forest Reserve

Kennisis River

Lake Definition

Elevation:	338 m (1,127 ft)
Surface Area:	38 ha (95 ac)
Mean Depth:	8.7 m (29.1 ft)
Max Depth:	38.1 m (127 ft)
Perimeter:	20 km (13 mi)
Way Point:	45° 12' 00" Lat - N
	78° 42' 00" Lon - W

N

Scale

400m   0   400m   800m   1200m   1600m

Redstone Lake (North)

Access

Redstone Lake is a popular Cottage Country destination nestled between the town of Haliburton and the Haliburton Forest Reserve. One of the main public access points to the big lake is located along its southwestern shore. To reach the access point, follow Highway 118 to the Eagle Lake Road (County Road 14) and head north. About 2 km (1.2 mi) past Eagle Lake there is an access road that branches west to the boat launch site on Redstone Lake.

Fishing

With one look at the hydrographic chart for Redstone Lake, you will notice that this lake is very unique with a vast array of bottom structure. Numerous mid lake humps and shoals are evident and depending on the depth, attract both lake trout and smallmouth bass. Being part of the Trent Canal headwater system, Redstone Lake experiences significant water fluctuations throughout the spring to fall season. When fishing, be sure to keep this factor in mind, as sportfish, especially bass, will move from some areas depending on depth.

Smallmouth bass fishing can be good at times in this lake. Smallmouth average 0.5-1 kg (1-2 lbs) and can be found larger. Bass anglers should try off any of the shallower shoal areas found around the lake. Shoals in the 3-6 m (10-20ft) range can be productive, especially if there is weed or rock structure evident. Working a jig or crayfish imitation fly or lure can work quite well along these areas.

A natural strain of lake trout remains in Redstone Lake and fishing for these lakers is regarded as fair at best. Ice fishing for lake trout is the main method of finding these trout; however, spring trolling just after ice off can also work well. Practicing catch and release for these natural lake trout can go a long way in helping preserve this naturally strain. Watch for special regulations on this lake.

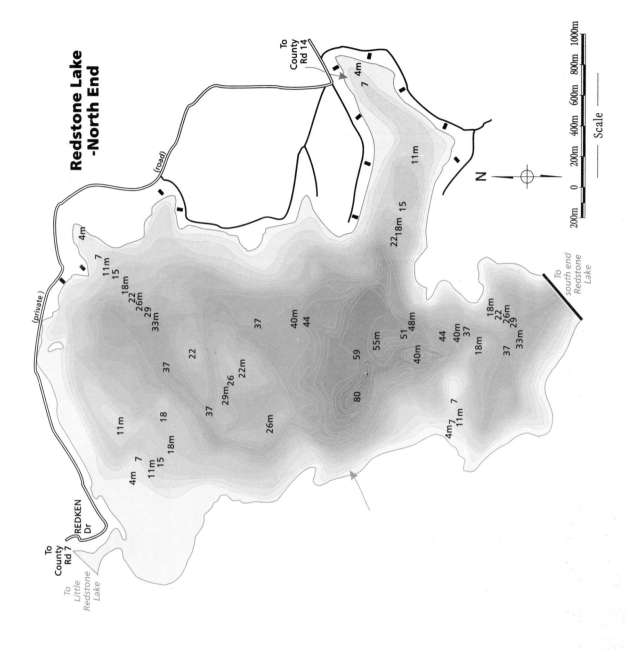

Redstone Lake
-North End

Redstone Lake (South)

Other Options

Little Redstone Lake is linked via a short channel to the much larger Redstone Lake and offers both lake trout and smallmouth bass. If you are looking for a little seclusion as an alternative to Redstone Lake, Guilford Lake can be reached by portage from the southwest shore of Redstone Lake. **Guilford Lake** is stocked periodically with splake and is a popular winter ice fishing destination.

Facilities

There are several camps and cottages on Redstone Lake, although the large lake remains generally quiet compared to many of the larger lakes in the region. For overnight accommodations, the area offers private campsites and resorts. Any needed supplies can be found in the town of Haliburton.

Haliburton

Redstone Lake ●
Dorset ● Haliburton ●
● Wilberforce
Minden ● ● Gooderham
Moore ● ● Kinmount
Falls
● Bobcaygean

Map Courtesy of Backroad Mapbook Cottage Country
Map 34/F5

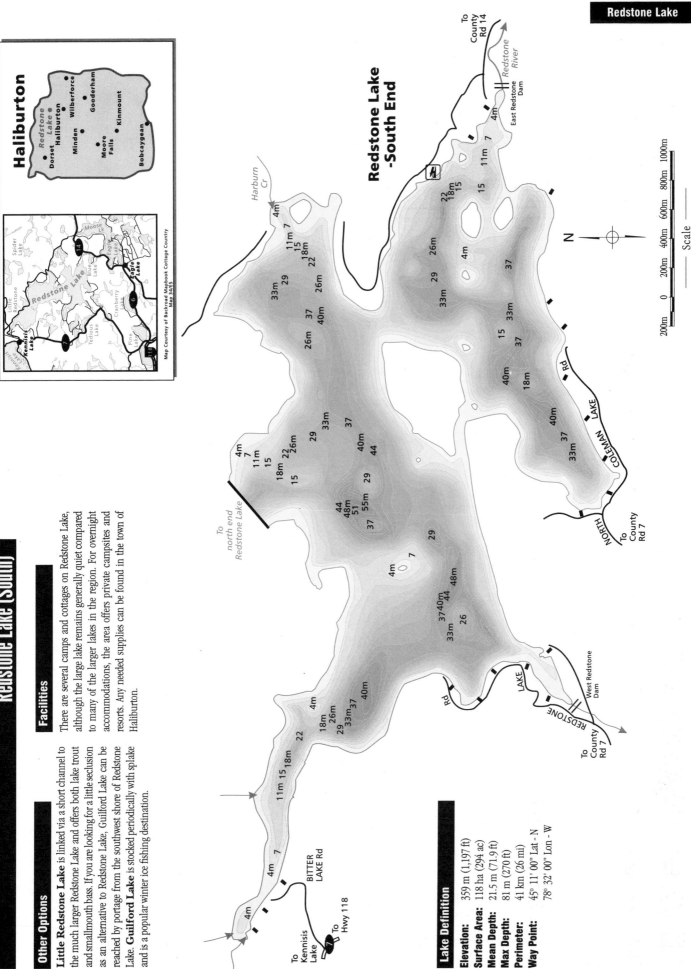

Redstone Lake
-South End

Lake Definition

Elevation:	359 m (1,197 ft)
Surface Area:	118 ha (294 ac)
Mean Depth:	21.5 m (71.9 ft)
Max Depth:	81 m (270 ft)
Perimeter:	41 km (26 mi)
Way Point:	45° 11' 00" Lat - N
	78° 32' 00" Lon - W

Scale

200m 0 200m 400m 600m 800m 1000m

Haliburton

- Dorset Haliburton
- Minden
- Wilberforce
- Gooderham
- *Rustyshoe Lake*
- Moore Falls
- Kinmount
- Bobcaygean

Rat Lakes

To Gooderham

To County Rd 36

507

Rustyshoe Lake

Map Courtesy of Backroad Mapbook Cottage Country Map 27/A1

Rustyshoe Lake

Access

South of the small village of Gooderham, Rustyshoe Lake can be found off the west side of Highway 507. A small boat access area is available just off the highway along the eastern shore of the lake.

Fishing

Due to the easy access and close proximity to Highway 507, Rustyshoe Lake does receive significant angling pressure throughout the year. However, fishing remains productive, as anglers can try their luck for smallmouth bass, largemouth bass, splake and the odd muskellunge.

Plenty of bass shoreline structure is found around the lake and working a jig or crayfish imitation fly or lure through the weeds and other natural structures can produce good results. Another lure that can work consistently is the spinner. Try casting spinners from a boat or canoe towards shore structure. Bass average around 0.5 kg (1 lb) in size in Rustyshoe Lake.

While fishing for bass, anglers are occasionally surprised by a musky strike, especially during the evening periods. Top water flies and lures can have success during the evening for bass and the odd musky. Cast along weed lines or even right in weed structure for top water action.

Splake are stocked in Rustyshoe Lake every few years and are most readily caught in the winter while ice fishing. In the spring, just after ice off, anglers can have success for splake by casting spinners and spoons, although the action slows considerably as the heat of summer approaches.

Other Options

Iron Lake and **Tamarack Lake** lie to the northeast of Rustyshoe Lake and are accessible via rough roads not far off Highway 507. Iron Lake is a small scenic lake that is surrounded by Crown Lake and is home to a small population of muskellunge. There are also reports of bass in the small lake. Tamarack Lake has a few camps along its shoreline and offers fishing opportunities for both largemouth and smallmouth bass.

Facilities

Outside of the access area, Rustyshoe Lake offers no facilities. The village of Gooderham lies minutes away to the north, while the town of Haliburton is about 30 minutes away. Overnight accommodations, restaurants and supplies can be found in and around these communities.

Lake Definition

Elevation:	302 m (1,006 ft)
Surface Area:	1 ha (3 ac)
Mean Depth:	7.5 m (25 ft)
Max Depth:	18.6 m (62 ft)
Perimeter:	3 km (2 mi)
Way Point:	44° 52' 00" Lat - N
	78° 24' 00" Lon - W

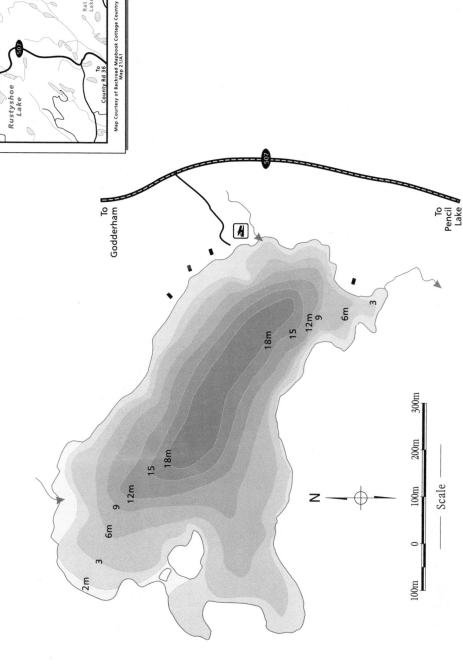

To Gooderham

507

To Pencil Lake

N

Scale

100m 0 100m 200m 300m

St. Nora Lake

Access

Highway 35 travels right past the main buildings of the Leslie M. Frost Centre, which is located along the western shore of St. Nora Lake. There is canoe access available from the Frost Centre area.

Fishing

The best action offered on St. Nora Lake is for its resident smallmouth bass. Smallmouth bass fishing can be good at times for bass that can reach over 1.5 kg (3.5 lbs). Spincasters should try using tube jigs or other type jigs. Fly anglers will find success with streamer patterns or a crayfish pattern worked close to bottom structure.

Anglers visiting St. Nora Lake can expect slow to fair success for natural lake trout. Ice fishing is the most productive time for finding lakers, although early spring just after ice off can also be decent. Before you head out on St. Nora Lake, please check the provincial fishing regulations as there are slot size restrictions for lake trout and ice fishing limits.

Other Options

If the action is slow on St. Nora, you can always portage into Sherborne Lake or paddle down to Kushog Lake. The centre **Sherborne Lake** can be reached via portage from the northeastern shore of St. Nora Lake, while a short channel connects St. Nora Lake to **Kushog Lake**. Both lakes offer fishing opportunities for lake trout and smallmouth bass.

Facilities

The Leslie M. Frost Centre is one of the main Ontario Ministry of Natural Resources training centres. The centre encompasses a large tract of land that contains numerous scenic interior lakes. Crown Land camping opportunities abound on the property and there are a few sites right on St. Nora Lake. For more information please contact the centre at (705) 766-2451 or visit their website at www.frostcentre.on.ca

Lake Definition

Elevation:	332 m (1,090ft)
Surface Area:	262 ha (647 ac)
Mean Depth:	15.7 m (51.5 ft)
Max Depth:	39.6 m (130 ft)
Perimeter:	17 km (11 mi)
Way Point:	45° 09' 00" Lat - N 78° 50' 00" Lon - W

Haliburton

Map Courtesy of Backroad Mapbook Cottage Country Map 26/E1

Depth Chart Not Intended for Navigational Use

89

Haliburton

• Dorset • Haliburton
  • Wilberforce
    • Minden • Gooderham
  • Moore   Salerno
    Falls   Lake
              • Kinmount

                    • Bobcaygean

Map Courtesy of Backroad Mapbook Cottage Country
Map 20/F1

Salerno Lake

Access

This long, boomerang shaped lake lies to the south of the settlement of Irondale. A few access roads branch south of Highway 503 and lead to the lake. The main access point is found at the Salerno Lake Dam, where there is a rough cartop type boat launch available.

Facilities

There are no facilities available at this lake other than the rustic access point.

Fishing

This shallow, brown coloured lake was once a fantastic fishery. Unfortunately, development has taken its toll as a number of cottages line the shoreline of Salerno Lake. However, the increased use of catch and release is starting to help improve the fishing quality of the lake over the past few years.

Anglers visiting Salerno Lake can expect to find mainly smallmouth and largemouth bass. Fishing for bass is fair and can be better on occasion for bass that can reach the 1.5 kg (3.5 lb) range. The shallow, weedy nature of the lake is prime habitat for bass and anglers should work weed areas for the best results. Try stripping a streamer pattern or a brighter coloured jig through the weeds for ambush ready bass. During slower times, a tube jig can work quite well.

Walleye fishing in Salerno Lake is definitely slower than success for bass. Walleye are the preferred sportfish of most anglers and can be found cruising the weed lines during the evening period. Trolling a worm harness slowly along these weed lines or still jigging off of a shoal can be effective. One hot spot for walleye is the 3 m (10 ft) shoal found in the southwestern end of the lake.

While muskellunge are present in Salerno Lake, the average angler may have a tough time finding them. Experienced musky hunters may find decent success on Salerno Lake, especially in the fall.

Other Options

To the east of Salerno Lake lies the remote access **Devils Gap Lake** and **Maple Lake**. Both lakes are quite secluded and offer fishing opportunities for smallmouth bass and largemouth bass. It is rumoured that Maple Lake also supports a population of walleye. Access to Devils Gap Lake is limited to a rough 4wd road/trail, while Maple Lake requires some bushwhacking to find.

Lake Definition

Elevation:	292 m (974 ft)
Surface Area:	14 ha (35 ac)
Mean Depth:	6 m (20 ft)
Max Depth:	13.2 m (44 ft)
Perimeter:	13 km (8 mi)
Way Point:	44° 51' 00" Lat - N
	78° 29' 00" Lon - W

Sherborne (Trout) Lake

Access

Set in the heart of the Leslie M. Frost Centre, Sherborne Lake can be reached by following Highway 35 to the Sherborne Road. The Sherborne Road is a rough forest access road that winds its way east, eventually reaching the northern shore of Sherborne Lake.

Other Options

While there are several lakes within portage access of Sherborne Lake, **Orley Lake** is one of the easier lakes to access. From the Sherborne Lake access point, the portage to Orley Lake lies just across the bay. The portage is a short 260 m (853 ft) walk up to the small, secluded lake. The lake is stocked with splake and is best fished in the winter through the ice or in the spring just after ice off.

Fishing

With the help of a hydrographic chart, anglers can dramatically increase their success on Sherborne Lake. The underwater nature of the lake is unique, as there is a vast array of underwater shoals, rock piles and other structures. Both smallmouth bass and natural lake trout inhabit Sherborne Lake.

Fishing for bass is generally good for bass in the 1 kg (2 lb) range. A good way to find smallmouth is to locate underwater shoals and rock structures. Smallmouth will congregate around these areas in the 3-4 m (10-13 ft) range. On occasion, they can be found as deep as 6 m (20 ft). Jigging off these areas or working a streamer type fly can produce quality results.

Lake trout continue to maintain a natural population in Sherborne Lake despite increased angling pressure on the species. During early spring, lakers can be found closer to the surface and can even be caught by spincasting. However later in the spring, lakers retreat to the deeper water and anglers must fish deeper.

In order to help protect the fragile lake trout population, Sherborne Lake is part of the winter/spring fishing sanctuary. Check the regulations for details.

Facilities

At the access point, a rough boat launch is available suitable for smaller type trailers and cartop crafts. As a part of the Leslie M. Frost Centre, Sherborne Lake is home to thirteen user maintained Crown Land campsites. For more information please contact the centre at (705) 766-2451 or visit their website at www.frostcentre.on.ca.

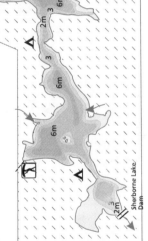

Lake Definition

Elevation: 358 m (1,175 ft)
Surface Area: 252 ha (622 ac)
Mean Depth: 9.5 m (31.3 ft)
Max Depth: 35 m (115 ft)
Perimeter: 24.6 km (15.3 mi)
Way Point: 45° 11' 00" Lat - N
78° 47' 00" Lon - W

To Hwy 35
SHERBORNE Rd
To Orley Lake
Shoelace Creek
Leslie M. Frost Centre
Falls
To Big Lake
Sherborne Lake Dam

Scale
200m 0 200m 400m 600m 800m 1000m

N

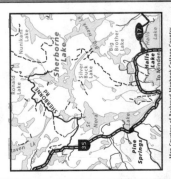

Haliburton

Dorset
Sherborne Lake
Haliburton
Wilberforce
Minden
Gooderham
Moore Falls
Kinmount
Bobcaygeon

Ronald Lake
Nunikani
Big Brother Lake
Sherborne Lake
Silver Buck Lake
Raven Lk
Halls Lake
To Minden
St Nora Lake
Pine Springs
35
17

91

South Lake

Access

East of the town of Minden, South Lake can be reached via County Road 16. The County Road branches east off Highway 35 and runs past the north end of the lake. There is no public access available on South Lake; however, there are a few privately run campgrounds on the lake that offer water access for a fee.

Lake Definition

Surface Area:	80 ha (198 ac)
Mean Depth:	7.3m (24 ft)
Max Depth:	11 m (36 ft)
Perimeter:	6 km (4 mi)
Way Point:	44° 55' 00" Lat - N
	78° 41' 00" Lon - W

Fishing

South Lake is a popular cottage destination lake that receives significant angling pressure throughout the season. The lake is generally quite shallow and offers fair fishing for smallmouth bass.

Bass are best found near weed structure, although they also frequent manmade structures such as boat docks. Try flipping a tube jig or casting a leech pattern close to these structures to entice smallmouth strikes. While the bass in South Lake are not very big, they always put up a commendable fight.

Facilities

Privately run campgrounds can be found around South Lake. Alternatively, the town of Minden is minutes away to the west via County Road 16. Visitors will find a number of restaurants, various retailers and accommodations as well as a Ministry of Natural Resources office in town.

Other Options

North of South Lake, **Bat Lake** is a decent fishing alternative. The smaller lake is found off a branch road from County Road 16 and offers decent angling opportunities for smallmouth bass.

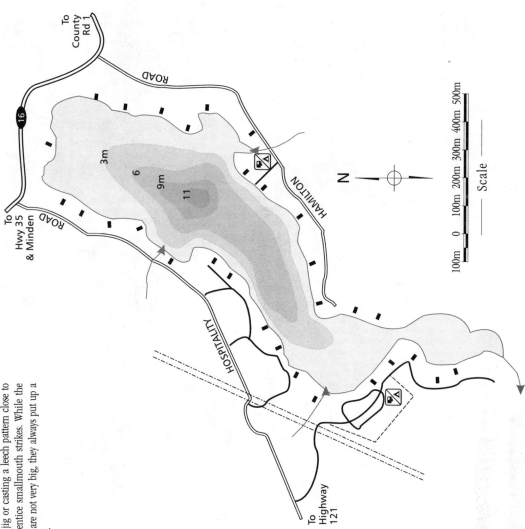

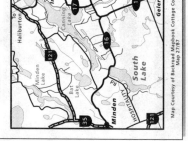

Map Courtesy of Backroad Mapbook Cottage Country
Map 27/87

Soyers Lake

Access

To reach Soyers Lake, follow Highway 121 south from the town of Haliburton. Approximately 10 km (6.2 mi) south of Haliburton, a boat launch can be found off the north side of Highway 121.

Lake Definition

Elevation: 323 m (1,076 ft)
Surface Area: 33 ha (83 ac)
Mean Depth: 18.6 m (62.3 ft)
Max Depth: 48 m (160 ft)
Perimeter: 16.8 km (10.5 mi)
Way Point: 45° 01' 00" Lat - N
78° 37' 00" Lon - W

Fishing

Anglers visiting Soyers Lake have the opportunity to fish for smallmouth bass, largemouth bass, walleye and natural lake trout. Fishing success is best for bass, as these aggressive sportfish are readily found along shore structure around the lake. Bass average approximately 1 kg (2 lbs) in size, although can be found larger. One particular holding area for bass is the bay in the northern end of the lake.

Walleye were originally introduced into Kashagawigamog Lake to the south of Soyers Lake. Soon after this introduction, walleye began appearing in Soyers Lake and have since developed a sustained population. Fishing success for walleye is generally fair for decent sized fish. Still jigging off drop-off areas can be productive, but trolling can be equally effective.

The lake trout of Soyers Lake are a naturally reproducing strain and fishing can be fair at times, although is often slow. Ice fishing is a popular activity on this lake as anglers can focus their efforts for both walleye and lake trout. However, check the regulations before heading out. There are slot size and ice fishing restrictions in place to aid walleye and lake trout stocks. Practicing catch and release can go a long way in maintaining this fishery.

Other Options

Due north of Soyers Lake anglers can find the secluded **Little Soyers Lake**. Access to the smaller lake is via a rough 4wd road and the effort is often rewarded with decent fishing for its resident smallmouth bass.

Facilities

Soyers Lake lies in between the towns of Minden to the south and Haliburton to the north. Both towns are minutes away and offer a variety of various amenities, including accommodations, restaurants and retailers.

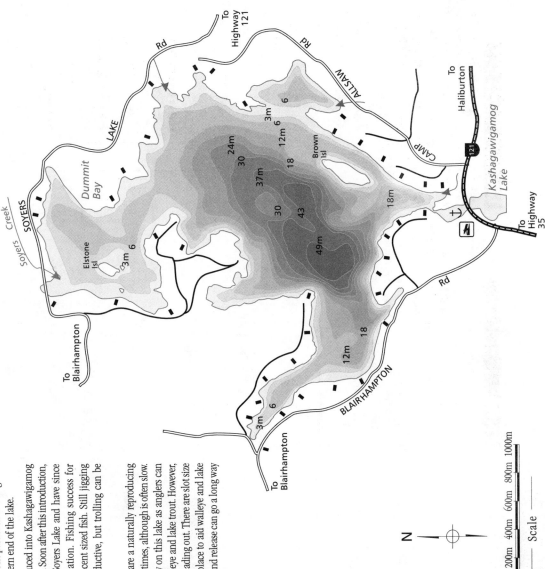

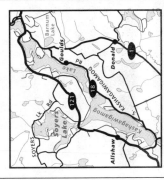

Map Courtesy of Backroad Mapbook Cottage Country Map 27/C4

Scale
200m   0   200m   400m   600m   800m   1000m

Stocking Lake

Access

Stocking Lake lies within the northwestern boundary of the beautiful Haliburton Forest Reserve. To find the lake, follow the Kennisis Lake Road (County Road 7) north off Highway 118 to the Haliburton Forest Reserve. Continue north along the Kennisis Lake Road to Kelly Road. Follow Kelly Road north to Stocking Lake Road, which travels west to the southern shore of the lake.

Fishing

Set in an isolated part of the Haliburton Forest Reserve, this scenic lake is inhabited by natural populations of brook trout and lake trout. Fishing for both species is regarded as fair to good at times and is best early in the season and later in the year. Lake trout in Stocking Lake are generally small, although there are some nice sized brookies caught regularly.

While trolling is the preferred method used by many anglers who visit Stocking Lake, simply casting a spinner from shore in the spring can be effective. Some anglers also find success with the basic bobber and worm, although patience is certainly required for this method to be successful. There are some prominent holes located around the lake and anglers are well advised to troll or cast around these areas to find these sometimes elusive trout.

Be sure to check the provincial fishing regulations summary before fishing. There are a number of restrictions including a winter sanctuary period, bait ban and slot size restrictions on brook trout.

Lake Definition

Surface Area: 93 ha (230 ac)
Mean Depth: 9 m (30 ft)
Max Depth: 18 m (60 ft)
Way Point: 45° 17' 00" Lat - N
78° 41' 00" Lon - W

Facilities

Being a rather secluded lake, there are no established facilities at Stocking Lake. Anglers will find an area where it is possible to launch small boats along the southern shore of the lake. Visitors to the area will find the Haliburton Forest Reserve is a wonderful year round outdoor recreation area. Facilities include a main lodge and cabin accommodations, a basic general store and camping. For more information on the Haliburton Forest, check out www.haliburtonforest.com.

Other Options

Just to the north of Stocking Lake, **Slipper Lake** can be reached via a short portage. The lake lies outside of the Haliburton Forest and anglers can expect to find similar fishing opportunities as in Stocking Lake. Both lake trout and brook trout inhabit Slipper Lake in decent numbers and are best caught early in the season. Watch for special restrictions.

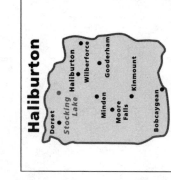

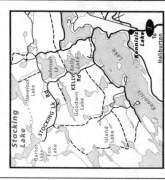

Map Courtesy of Backroad Mapbook Cottage Country Map 34/A5

Scale

100m 0 100m 200m 300m 400m 500m

To Slipper Lake

To Johnson Lake

STOCKING LAKE Rd

Haliburton Forest Reserve

N

94

Stormy Lake

Access

Stormy Lake can be found by following Highway 121 east from Haliburton to Buckhorn Road (County Road 3). Head south along Buckhorn Road and look for the south Stormy Lake Road. The south Stormy Lake Road leads to the southern end of the lake and a public access area.

Fishing

This rusty coloured lake does not look like a lake that would be home to trout species, but a natural population of lake trout roams the lake. Fishing pressure on these lake trout has been quite consistent in the past and anglers will currently find slow fishing. With the closure of ice fishing on Stormy Lake, it is hoped that the lake trout population will eventually rebound.

Anglers looking for some decent action out on Stormy Lake are best to visit the lake in the summer and try for its resident smallmouth bass. Fishing for smallmouth bass up to 1.5 kg (3.5 lbs) is regarded as fair. Bass are best caught along shore structure using deep prodding flies and lures. Try casting a bright coloured jig or spinner off rock points around the lake for aggressive smallmouth.

Before heading out on Stormy Lake, be sure to check the fishing regulations summary as there is a winter sanctuary period imposed on the lake to aid fragile lake trout stocks.

Other Options

There are a number of angling alternatives nearby Stormy Lake, including the **Glamor Lakes** to the east of Stormy Lake. The Glamor Lakes are accessible via a 2wd road and offer fishing opportunities mainly for smallmouth bass. The larger Glamor Lake is also home to a population of lake trout and has been recently stocked with rainbow trout. Watch for special restrictions on these lakes.

Facilities

There is a rough public boat launch available along the southern shore of Stormy Lake. The village of Haliburton is a bustling summer town that offers area visitors all necessary supplies and amenities.

Recent Fish Stocking

Year	Fish Species
1996	Lake trout

Lake Definition

Elevation:	372 m (1,240 ft)
Surface Area:	5 ha (13 ac)
Mean Depth:	8.4 m (28 ft)
Max Depth:	24 m (80 ft)
Perimeter:	5.4 km (3.4 mi)
Way Point:	44° 58' 00" Lat - N
	78° 24' 00" Lon - W

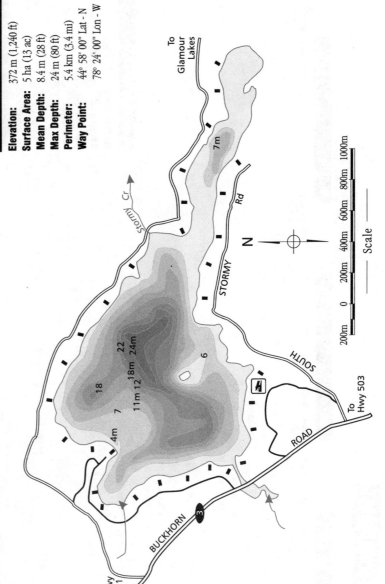

Map Courtesy of Backroad Mapbook Cottage Country Map 27/65

Tedious (Long) Lake

Access

To reach Tedious Lake, follow Highway 118 to the Kennisis Lake Road (County Road 7) and head north. The Kennisis Lake Road soon passes by the western shore of the lake and a boat launch.

Fishing

Tedious Lake is stocked annually with lake trout, which provide for good fishing at times during the winter months. Ice fishing off shoals with small spoons or light coloured jigs can work quite well. Presenting these lures in the upper portion of the lake is your best bet for a lake trout strike through the ice. After ice off, lakers can be found almost anywhere around the lake and can be caught by regular spincasting techniques.

Smallmouth bass also inhabit Tedious Lake and provide fair fishing throughout the summer months. The shallower portions of the lake are the best holding areas for smallmouth. Look for smallies in weed structure and in approximately the 4-6 m (13-20 ft) range. Work flies, jigs and spinners along structure to entice hard smallmouth strikes.

Other Options

Bitter Lake and **Burdock Lake** lie just to the north of Tedious Lake and are both accessible via rough 2wd roads. Burdock Lake is stocked with brook trout, while Bitter Lake is stocked regularly with lake trout. Fishing in both lakes is productive, especially in the winter through the ice.

Facilities

Other than its public access area, there are no facilities at Tedious Lake.

Lake Definition

Surface Area: 30 ha (73 ac)
Mean Depth: 4.8 m 16 ft)
Max Depth: 22 m (72 ft)
Way Point: 45° 10' 00" Lat - N
78° 35' 00" Lon - W

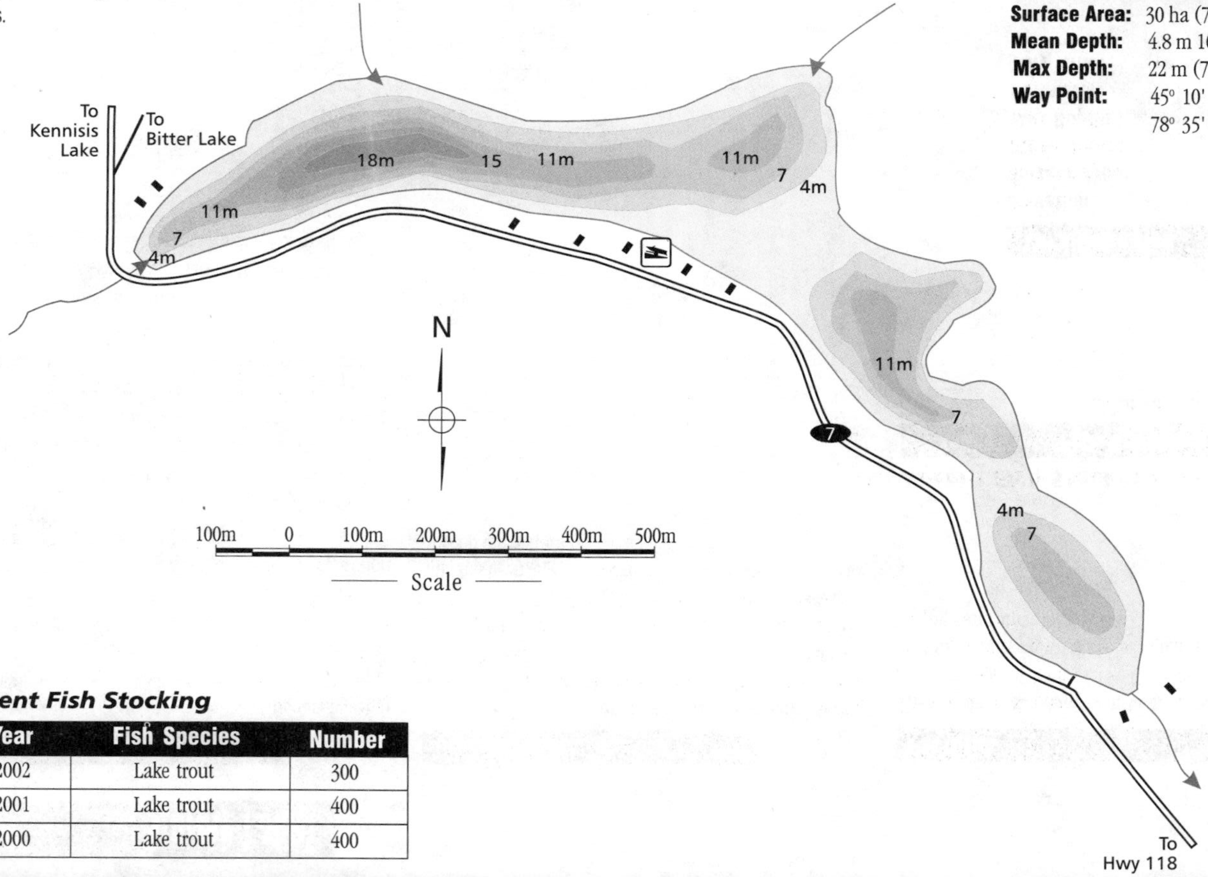

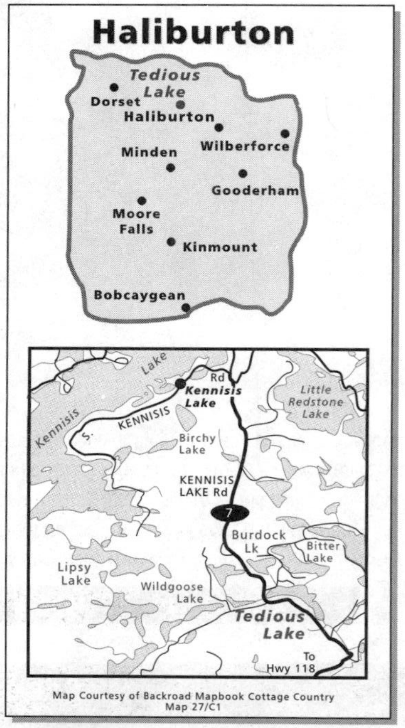

Recent Fish Stocking

Year	Fish Species	Number
2002	Lake trout	300
2001	Lake trout	400
2000	Lake trout	400

Map Courtesy of Backroad Mapbook Cottage Country
Map 27/C1

Haliburton

Troutspawn (Big Trout) Lake

Access

This secluded lake lies to the south of Algonquin Park's West Gate. Many anglers access Troutspawn Lake from the south by following County Road 12 northeast from Dorset. At the end of the road, follow the west branch to the shore of Troutspawn Lake. It is also possible to make your way southeast from Highway 60 west of Algonquin Park.

Due to the remote location, it is a good idea to bring along a good road map such as those found in the Backroad Mapbook for Cottage Country Ontario. In addition to detailed road and trail maps, there is valuable information on hundreds of lakes, paddling routes, parks and much more.

Fishing

Troutspawn Lake is also known as Big Trout Lake, which certainly entices most anglers into wanting to test their luck. Unfortunately, most of the angling attention comes from the local cottage owners and reports out of the lake vary.

Troutspawn Lake was stocked some time ago with brook trout. There was also a natural population of brookies in the lake, but it is currently unclear if brook trout remain in the lake. If you are in the area, this lake is one of those beautiful mysterious lakes that may provide some exciting spring and fall trout fishing.

Other Options

There is plenty of angling options around Troutspawn Lake, such as **Little Troutspawn Lake** and the **Louie Lakes** to the south. Little Troutspawn Lake is stocked periodically with brook trout, while the two Louie Lakes are rumoured to continue to support natural brook trout populations. The larger Louie Lake has also been stocked with splake in the past.

Facilities

As a secluded lake, there are very little in the way of facilities available. There is, however, a rough launching area and Crown Land camping opportunities. Supplies can be found in the village of Dorset.

Lake Definition

Elevation:	409 m (1,341 ft)
Surface Area:	99 ha (245 ac)
Mean Depth:	5.1 m (16.9 ft)
Max Depth:	13.7 m (45 ft)
Perimeter:	7 km (4 mi)
Way Point:	45° 24' 00" Lat - N
	78° 45' 00" Lon - W

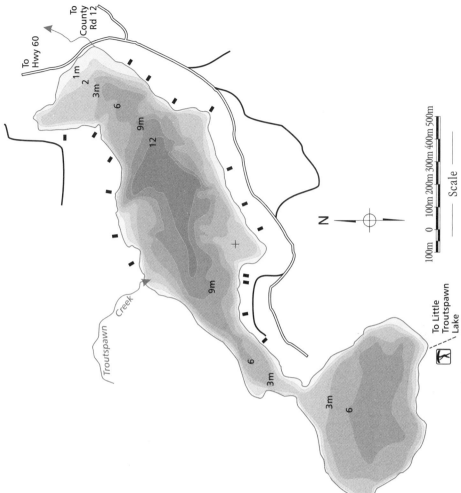

Depth Chart Not Intended for Navigational Use

Map Courtesy of Backroad Mapbook Cottage Country Map 33/f2

Map Labels

To Maple Lake

118

Carnarvon

Tall Pines Cottages

Mac ARTHUR Rd

35

Twelve Mile Lake Dam

To Minden

4
7m
11
15m
18
21m
18
15m
11
7m
4
4
4

HOUSE Rd

TAYLOR Rd

12m
6
3m
2m

Woit's Pt

CROOKED

TOWN LOT Rd

118

To Brady Lake

Boshkung Lake

Little Boshkung Lake

Twelve Mile Lake

N

Scale

200m   0   200m 400m 600m 800m 1000m

Twelve Mile & Little Boshkung Lakes

Access

Little Boshkung and Twelve Mile Lake are interconnected lakes and are found a few minutes north of the town of Minden. There are two main access points on Twelve Mile Lake, one on its southern end and one along the eastern shore of the lake. Both access sites can be reached off of Highway 35. A boat launch can also be found near the northern shore of Little Boshkung Lake off Highway 118.

Other Options

Sharron Lake and **Gray Lake** are two small lakes that offer decent angling alternatives. Sharron Lake can be accessed off the east side of Highway 35 and is home to a population of smallmouth bass. Gray Lake is accessible via Queens Line Road west of Little Boshkung Lake. Both smallmouth bass and largemouth bass inhabit Gray Lake. Please do not trespass.

Fishing

As one of the larger and easier accessible lakes in the area, Twelve Mile Lake does receive plenty of angling attention throughout the year. The same holds true for Little Boshkung Lake, since it is connected to Twelve Mile Lake. Both lakes continue to provide consistent results for smallmouth bass and lake trout.

Fishing is best for resident bass. Smallmouth can be found in the 1.5 kg (3.5 lb) range, although they are caught larger on occasion. The key to smallmouth success is to work the drop-offs and bottom areas. Bouncing a tube jig off bottom structure is a proven method for finding scrappy smallies in these lakes. During slow periods, try slowing the presentation down.

Lake trout fishing is regarded as fair at times but it can be quite slow, especially during the summer months. Ice fishing is perhaps the most productive method for these lakers. In winter, it is best to focus efforts off shoals in the upper portion of the lake. Slot size and special ice fishing restrictions are in place on these lakes to help the natural lake trout species survive. Be sure to check the regulations for details.

Facilities

Tall Pines Housekeeping Cottages offer 2 and 3 bedroom self catering cottages nestled amongst tall pine trees overlooking Twelve Mile Lake. They provide docking facilities, boat rentals as well as the use of a paddle boat and canoe. Their central location also allows guests to walk to restaurants, mini golf and other activities, while the villages of Haliburton and Minden are close by. Visit www.tallpinescottages.com or call 1-705-489-3739.

Lake Definition

Elevation:	303 m (1,010 ft)
Surface Area:	33 ha (82 ac)
Mean Depth:	11.8 m (39.4 ft)
Max Depth:	27 m (90.0 ft)
Perimeter:	12 km (8 mi)
Way Point:	45° 01' 00" Lat - N
	78° 43' 00" Lon - W

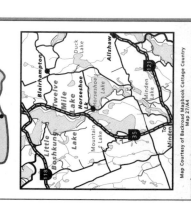

Haliburton

Dorset • Twelve Mile Lake
• Haliburton
• Wilberforce
Minden • Gooderham
Moore • Kinmount
Falls
• Bobcaygeon

Blairhampton
Duck Lake
Twelve Mile Lake
Allshaw
121
Horseshoe Lake
Mountain Lake
Minden
35
Little Boshkung Lake
118
To Minden

Map Courtesy of Backroad Mapbook Cottage Country Map 27/A4

Two Island (East) Lake

Access

Also known as East Lake, this lake has two prominent islands that help give it a unique character. To reach the lake, follow Highway 121 east from the town of Haliburton to East Bay Road. East Bay Road travels north from the highway, eventually passing by the western end of the lake. While there is no official access to the lake, it is possible to launch a canoe from the side of the road.

Fishing

Anglers visiting Two Island Lake can expect to find a good population of smallmouth bass as well as a fair population of natural lake trout. Fishing for smallmouth is best during overcast or the evening periods as the clear nature of the lake can spook smallmouth during bright days. Regardless of the day, try working your presentations deep around rock structures. The areas just off the two islands can hold a number of bass. Fly anglers should try a darker coloured streamer pattern like a wooly bugger or a crayfish imitation. For spincasters, spinners can create results but jigs are often your best bet.

Since the season for lake trout begins later in the year, lake trout are often already holding in the deeper areas of the lake. Hence, trolling is the main method of finding lake trout throughout the year. Downrigging equipment is not necessary, although it definitely increases the chances of success. Try working small to medium sized silver spoons deep to entice lake trout strikes. Two Island Lake is part of the winter/spring fishing sanctuary in order to help maintain natural lake trout populations. Please practice catch and release.

Facilities

The nearby town of Haliburton is the focal point of the region and is a fantastic place to visit throughout the year. All amenities like restaurants and accommodations are available in this small Ontario tourist town.

Other Options

En route to Two Island Lake you will pass by **South Portage Lake**. South Portage Lake is a popular summer destination that offers fishing opportunities for decent sized smallmouth and largemouth bass. There are also rumours of a small muskellunge population available in the lake.

Lake Definition

Elevation:	328 m (1,093 ft)
Surface Area:	5 ha (13 ac)
Mean Depth:	6 m (20 ft)
Max Depth:	21 m (70 ft)
Perimeter:	5 km (3 mi)
Way Point:	45° 04' 00" Lat - N
	78° 22' 00" Lon - W

Recent Fish Stocking

Year	Fish Species
1999	Splake
1997	Splake
1995	Splake

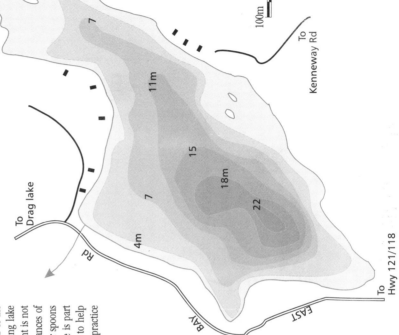

Two Island Lake

N

Scale

100m 0 100m 200m 300m 400m 500m

To Kenneway Rd

To Drag lake

Bay Rd

To Hwy 121/118

EAST BAY

4m

7

11m

15

7

18m

22

4m

Haliburton

Two Island Lake

Dorset • Haliburton • Wilberforce
Minden • Gooderham
Moore Falls • Kinmount
Bobcaygeon

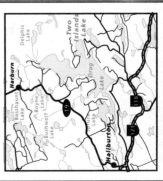

Delphis Lake

Two Islands Lake

Harburn

Drag Lake

Basshaun Lake

Boyne Lake

19

Bushwolf Lake

118

Haliburton

121

Map Courtesy of Backroad Mapbook Cottage Country
Map 28/A3

Wilbermere Lake

Haliburton

Wilbermere Lake

- Dorset Haliburton
- Wilberforce
- Gooderham
- Minden
- Moore Falls
- Kinmount
- Bobcaygean

Map Courtesy of Backroad Mapbook Cottage Country Map 28/E4

Huckleberry Lake

Wilbermere Lake

Buckskin Lake

Lower Buckskin Lake

Monrock Lake

Ted's Lake

South Wilberforce

To Halliburton

Lake Definition

Elevation: 340 m (1,133 ft)
Surface Area: 4 ha (10 ac)
Mean Depth: 6.9 m (23 ft)
Max Depth: 21.6 m (72 ft)
Perimeter: 6 km (4 mi)
Way Point: 45° 00' 00" Lat - N
78° 13' 00" Lon - W

Recent Fish Stocking

Year	Fish Species	Number
2002	Lake trout	500
2001	Lake trout	600
2000	Lake trout	600

Access

Wilbermere Lake can be reached by following Highway 121 east from the village of Tory Hill to Highway 648. About 4 km (2.5 mi) north along the smaller highway, look for Wilbermere Lake off the east side of the road.

Fishing

Wilbermere Lake is stocked annually with lake trout, which provide for fair fishing that can be good on occasion. Lake trout average approximately 35 cm (14 in) in size and are best caught in the winter through the ice. When ice fishing, try jigging in 5-10 m (16-32 ft) of water, but work your lure in the upper half of this depth. Lakers will often cruise around in this upper layer, due mainly to the fact that oxygen levels are best in this region.

Fair populations of smallmouth bass also inhabit the lake and frequent the shoreline areas. Flipping jigs, spinners and streamer type flies along shore structure can provide results for aggressive smallies. When smallmouth are lethargic, try slowing the presentation down to entice strikes.

Other Options

A decent alternative to Wilbermere Lake is Monrock Lake. **Monrock Lake** can be found by taking Highway 121 east of Tory Hill to the Rock Lake Road. The Rock Lake Road treks south past the eastern end of the lake. Monrock Lake offers consistent angling opportunities for smallmouth bass.

Facilities

There are a number of privately run campgrounds available around Wilbermere Lake, while the nearby village of Tory Hill offers basic amenities.

To County Rd 4

To Hwy 121

648

South Wilberforce

To Hwy 648

3m
6
9m
12
15m
18

3m
6
9m
12
15m
18

N

Scale

100m 0 100m 200m 300m 400m 500m

Wren Lake

Access

Wren Lake lies within the Leslie M. Frost Centre, although there are a few cottages along its shoreline. The lake can be reached by following Highway 35 north past the Frost Centre administration buildings. The lake lies off the west side of the highway and it is possible to launch a canoe off the side of the highway.

Facilities

The Leslie M. Frost Centre is a scenic Crown Land area that offers backcountry camping on several of its lakes. Although none are found on Wren Lake, ambitious paddlers can reach a number of backcountry lakes in the area. For more information, call (705) 766-2451 or visit their website at www.frostcentre.on.ca.

Fishing

Wren Lake was originally named Three Mile Lake, although with the popularity of the 'Three Mile Lake' name, the lake was later changed to Wren Lake. The lake has never been known as a good fishing lake, although over the past few decades, fishing quality has improved significantly.

Like many lakes in the region, smallmouth bass were introduced in Wren Lake over twenty years ago and have since established a naturally regenerating population. Fishing for smallmouth is fair for bass that average 0.5-1 kg (1-2 lbs) in size. Bass in this lake are difficult to coax to the top, as the clarity of the water does make them cautious. The best method for finding these bass is to work the bottom structure with tube jigs or crayfish imitation type flies.

Splake are heavily stocked in Wren Lake and provide for good fishing at times for the brook trout/lake trout hybrid. Ice fishing is the most productive time of year for splake, although they can also be caught readily during the spring. Spoons and flashy spinners are the best choice for finding splake.

Other Options

To the north of Wren Lake, **Grindstone Lake** is accessible via a short portage. There are a few cottages and camps along its shoreline, but the lake remains another peaceful Leslie M. Frost Centre lake. Grindstone Lake is stocked every few years with splake.

Lake Definition

Elevation: 345 m (1,150 ft)
Surface Area: 5 ha (13 ac)
Mean Depth: 4.6 m (15.4 ft)
Max Depth: 12.3 m (41 ft)
Perimeter: 7 km (4 mi)
Way Point: 45° 11' 00" Lat - N
78° 52' 00" Lon - W

Recent Fish Stocking

Year	Fish Species	Number
2002	splake	1,200
2001	Splake	2,100
1999	Splake	2,100

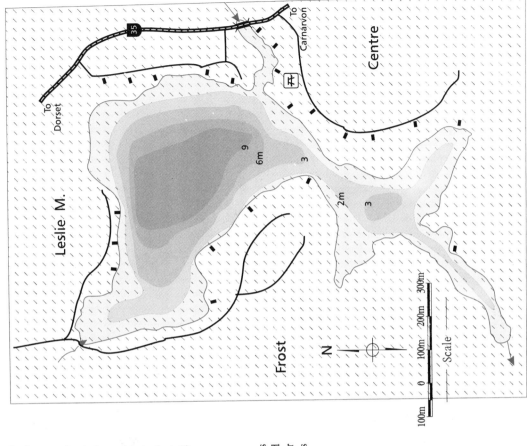

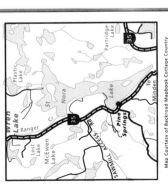

Map Courtesy of Backroad Mapbook Cottage Country Map 26/D1

Ontario's Important Numbers

Ministry of Natural Resources

General Inquiry ....(800) 667-1940

...............................(800) 667-1840 (French)

..................e-mail: mnr.nric@mnr.gov.on.ca

Outdoors Card (Licenses, Customer Service) ....(800) 387-7011

Aurora, Greater Toronto Area ....

....(905) 713-7400

 Algonquin.....................(613) 637-2780

 Bracebridge.................(705) 645-8747

 Minden.........................(705) 286-1521

Parks

Reservations ....(888) ONT-PARK

..........................www.ontarioparks.com

Algonquin.............................(705) 633-5572

Silent Lake ....(613) 339-2807

Crime Stoppers (Poaching) ....

..........................(800) 222-TIPS (8477)

Invading Species Hotline ....

....(800) 563-7711

Sport Fish Contaminant Monitoring Programme ....(800) 820-2716

Updates ....

...............www.backroadmapbooks.com

Tourism, Resorts & Lodges

Ontario Tourism..............(800) ONT-ARIO

Resorts Ontario ....(705) 325-9115

Help Us Help You

A comprehensive resource such as **FISHING ONTARIO** could not be put together without a great deal of help and support. Despite our best efforts to ensure that everything is accurate, errors do occur. If you see any errors or omissions, please continue to let us know.

Mail to:

Mussio Ventures Ltd.

232 Anthony Court

New Westminster, B.C. V3L 5T5

All updates will be posted on our website: **www.backr oadmapbooks.com**

Phone: 1-877-520-5670

Fax: 1-604-438-3470

Email: updates@backroadmapbooks.com